Start with Welcome combines biblical
on how we can follow Jesus in seeing t.
to make invisible.

RUSSELL MOORE, editor in chief, *Christianity Today*

If you are curious what Scripture teaches about how to care for the immigrant and refugee in an incredibly complex world, there is no better place to start than this book.

SHARON HODDE MILLER, author of *The Cost of Control*

Bri Stensrud courageously decided some years ago that—because immigration is not just a political issue but also a biblical issue impacting people fearfully and wonderfully made in God's image—she needed to engage. I'm so grateful she did.

MATTHEW SOERENS, vice president of advocacy and policy, World Relief

Bri Stensrud is an inspiring leader who responded to what she was seeing in the world around her, reading in her Bible, and discerning from the Holy Spirit. I hope her response will inspire readers to consider how God might be calling them to respond.

MICHAEL WEAR, founder, president, and CEO, The Center for Christianity and Public Life, and author of *The Spirit of Our Politics*

Evil wants nothing more than to divide us and shift our posture from Jesus-like to worldly. I'm grateful for leaders like Bri, who is willing both to stand in the trenches of unity and also to hold out her hand and invite us all to do the same—as Jesus would.

TONI COLLIER, podcaster and author of *Brave Enough to Be Broken*

An inspiring call to embrace our immigrant neighbors with love, compassion, and understanding, *Start with Welcome* provides a more balanced and compassionate perspective on this critical conversation from a biblical perspective.

YONATHAN MOYA, founder and executive director, Border Perspective

Start with Welcome walks us through Scripture, stories, and statistics to help navigate the humanitarian crisis at our border. Bri demonstrates that we don't have to choose between secure borders and compassionate welcome to the "least of these" seeking hope and help.

KELLY ROSATI, former vice president of advocacy for children, Focus on the Family

Start with Welcome invites us to think well about immigration, with an understanding of the human dignity each person holds as an image bearer of God. This book helps believers wrestle with this complex topic in a truthful and empathetic way.

LAUREN GREEN MCAFEE, ministry director, Hobby Lobby Ministry Investments, and founder, Stand for Life

There is something life-changing about creating welcome for people. *Start with Welcome* attaches biblical confidence to our compassion and helps us get closer to those who have so much God-given potential.

JESSICA HONEGGER, founder, Noonday Collection

I am so excited for this book and the challenges it will bring to all of us. We need this fresh and biblical call to hospitality and compassion.

BRADY BOYD, pastor, New Life Church

In *Start with Welcome*, Bri invites us into a heartfelt conversation about a complex issue. She shows what it means to love our neighbors no matter their background or circumstance. It will leave you challenged, inspired, and forever changed.

ELIZABETH GRAHAM, CEO, Stand for Life

Bri Stensrud writes with theological depth, practical experience, and—above all—humility. *Start with Welcome* is a gently courageous invitation to become what we are: a people glad to extend welcome because we serve a God who never stops welcoming us.

ANDREW ARNDT, lead pastor, New Life East

In a time and with a topic marked by hot-headed arguments or cold-shouldered dismissals, Bri Stensrud has given us a work of remarkable warmth—a warmth of compassion for people created in God's image, and a warmth of regard for you the reader to be dignified with thoughtful research on complex issues and thought-provoking explorations of Scripture. Start this journey of welcome with her and discover the radical warmth of Christ's hospitality.

WALTER KIM, president, National Association of Evangelicals

Bri gives us a broader range of options for a conversation that has been extreme on both sides. Nuanced, thoughtful, well-researched, appropriately provocative—*Start with Welcome* is a call to a more compassionate Christianity.

DANIEL GROTHE, pastor, New Life Church

start with welcome

The Journey toward a Confident and Compassionate Immigration Conversation

BRI STENSRUD

with Catherine McNiel

ZONDERVAN
REFLECTIVE

ZONDERVAN REFLECTIVE

Start with Welcome
Copyright © 2024 by Bri Stensrud

Published in Grand Rapids, Michigan, by Zondervan. Zondervan is a registered trademark of The Zondervan Corporation, L.L.C., a wholly owned subsidiary of HarperCollins Christian Publishing, Inc.

Requests for information should be addressed to customercare@harpercollins.com.

Zondervan titles may be purchased in bulk for educational, business, fundraising, or sales promotional use. For information, please email SpecialMarkets@Zondervan.com.

ISBN 978-0-310-15427-3 (audio)

Library of Congress Cataloging-in-Publication Data

Names: Stensrud, Bri, author.
Title: Start with welcome : the journey toward a confident and compassionate immigration conversation / Bri Stensrud.
Description: Grand Rapids : Zondervan, 2024.
Identifiers: LCCN 2023036273 (print) I LCCN 2023036274 (ebook) I ISBN 9780310154259 (paperback) I ISBN 9780310154266 (ebook)
Subjects: LCSH: Emigration and immigration—Religious aspects—Christianity. I Hospitality—Religious aspects—Christianity. I BISAC: RELIGION / Christian Living / Social Issues I RELIGION / Christian Living / Women's Interests
Classification: LCC BR115.E45 S74 2024 (print) I LCC BR115.E45 (ebook) I DDC 261.8/38—dc23/eng/20230927
LC record available at https://lccn.loc.gov/2023036273
LC ebook record available at https://lccn.loc.gov/2023036274

Published in association with the literary agent Don Gates at The Gates Group.

Cover design: Emily Weigel Design
Cover photography: Shutterstock
Interior design: Kait Lamphere

Printed in the United States of America

23 24 25 26 27 LBC 5 4 3 2 1

For my sisters in Christ who keep showing up
to love people in the hard and messy margins
of life. Let's keep going. I'm with you.

And to my wonderful family, whose support allows me
to say yes to the things God calls me to. I love you.

contents

foreword

Over the last couple of years, my idea of what it means to be "pro-life" has been shattered to pieces. Growing up, *pro-life* meant that someone was against abortion. As a follower of Jesus, I believe that life begins at conception, and there isn't a circumstance in which that life would not have value. Therefore, I am a faithful pro-lifer.

However, this idea of what it means to be pro-life has been tested for me personally in the last few years. Many circumstances, conversations, and interactions have shone a bright light on how shallow my pro-life narrative was. For me, and maybe for many of you, it was all about the unborn. How are we caring for the unborn? What are we doing to make abortion illegal? How do we stop the death of so many unborn children in our country? These were the only questions I heard being asked, and therefore, they were all I thought about when it came to pro-life issues.

But then, through various events, I drew closer to other life issues. I began volunteering at a local high school's teen mom program. There, I saw many amazing, strong, beautiful girls who had chosen life for their children. Yes! They were pro-life like me! But though they had made the beautiful decision to carry their babies to term, their lives were very hard and they needed so much help. By walking alongside them, I saw firsthand that pro-life issues go beyond the child in the womb. Who was looking out for these girls? Where was the help for them now that many of them were single teen moms? As the church, we would celebrate these children not being aborted, but then what were we doing for these moms? It seemed like we were telling them to pull themselves up by their bootstraps and figure things out on their own. For me, the narrative around being pro-life began to widen. Being pro-life had to include supporting women too.

Our family spent a few years living in an under-resourced neighborhood in Austin, Texas, where I came face-to-face with people who had struggles in life that I'd never had to overcome as a middle-class white woman. Some of them were living in the US with a green card, and some were without legal documentation. Real people. My neighbors. Hardworking men and women who wanted the best for their families. This, too, challenged my single-issue pro-life narrative. Being pro-life had to include supporting my neighbors who were undocumented.

A few years ago, I met a college student who was a DACA recipient (Deferred Action for Childhood Arrivals—a program created to help children who were brought to the US by their parents). She said she was worried about her ability to finish nursing school because she wasn't sure what the government would do with her status as a citizen. I had never met anyone in that situation. She had lived in the US almost her whole life and was studying on an academic scholarship, but now she was losing sleep worrying about her future. My proximity to her story widened my pro-life narrative. It had to include supporting DACA kids.

In 2019 I was invited to go on a trip to the US-Mexico border with my friends from Women of Welcome and World Relief. I was excited and curious. The media was spinning a narrative, politicians were too, and I wanted to see and hear what was really happening with my own eyes and ears. Listening to stories about exhausting journeys to the US to escape unspeakable violence and corruption continued to challenge my narrow view of being pro-life. Leaving El Paso, I was reminded that the life of every single asylum seeker and immigrant matters to God, and therefore, they should matter to me as well.

These experiences, plus more that I don't have room for on these pages, have changed my heart about being pro-life. I'm still a pro-life evangelical Christian. That hasn't changed. What has changed is how I define *pro-life*. I'm still against abortion and believe that every child matters, has value, and should be given the right to life. I also believe that *every* person who is already breathing matters and should be valued. Every person has a dignity given to them by our Creator, and we need to acknowledge that and apply it to their lives. This truth should change the way we treat people and talk about them. It should change the way we vote and which policies matter to us.

Over the last few years, as I have leaned in and listened more about these issues, Bri has been a lifeline for me. She has encouraged me and taught me. She has cried with me and been angry with me. She has allowed my journey to unfold in its own time and been gracious with my questions and fears. If you, too, are willing to lean in, listen a bit more, and get a little more uncomfortable, I believe your heart, too, can start to ache more for the least of these. If you let him, the Holy Spirit will move and convict and guide and take you in a more Christlike and loving direction than you may have ever experienced before. I'm so grateful for Bri, her leadership, and her wisdom, and I will be telling people to read this book for many years to come. I'm excited for you to dive in and see how *Start with Welcome* changes the whole conversation!

Jamie Ivey

introduction

Conversations about immigration can be intimidating. But hopefully after reading this book, you won't be afraid to have them. Great books on immigration are already floating about in the world, so here's my confession, right at the top: this book is not going to be a complete account of everything the Bible says on immigration. I'm not going to cram in an explanation of every immigration policy that's been passed or is needed (although I will talk about that a bit). This book is meant to be an easy-ish conversation about a hard topic, a friendly conversation based in conviction and charitability. Hopefully it will recalibrate our hearts in Christ's direction and apply to more than just your journey into the US immigration and asylum system.

Contrary to what you might think, I'm not writing to twist your arm about such things. That's not my job. I don't expect you to believe exactly what I do. But I want to consider some important things together. I've spent hours upon hours pretending you were on the other side of my laptop having tea or coffee with me, imagining us sitting down for a gracious and honest chat about the things that concern us, the headlines that scare us, and the images that have shifted our hearts.

Full transparency: I do have a goal for this book, but it's pretty painless.

My goal is simply not to leave you where you are.

What I want most is for all of us to see *people* first. To do this, we must get closer to the issue and, more importantly, to the people. Particularly, we need to get close to the neighbors we may have disregarded because of their circumstances, the way they came to our communities, or their lack of proper documentation. Perhaps you're afraid—and maybe you have forgotten where that fear came from in the first place. We'll talk about all this too.

The conversation I want to have with you is challenging, but no one will be yelling. This isn't an argument or a game. It is more of a heart-to-heart for those of us who remain curious. We'll be challenged to choose people over politics, compassion over comfort, and welcome over worry. You might already feel compassion for immigrants and refugees. If so, this book aims to attach confidence to that compassion—to help you feel seen, assure you that you're not crazy or alone, and give you confidence that your pursuit of proximity in this space is well justified and honoring to God. Others of you might be nervous, skeptical, or confused. Great! Come sit with me. You're in the right place. Stay curious, ask the hard questions, and keep going. God is not afraid of your doubts or your questions. He simply asks for a humble heart and a life willing to constantly recalibrate and reconnect with his mission to choose welcome for "the least of these."

For as we've done unto them, we have done unto Christ himself (Matt. 25:40).

Just writing that sentence sobers my mind in a fresh way. I hope reading it does the same for you. We're going on a journey together, and it doesn't matter to me where you land: that's between you and God. But I hope we'll learn new things together, grieve hard things together, and ask for forgiveness together when we realize we've missed the mark. This is a good conversation to have, and neither of us is alone in wondering where to go with all this God-given compassion.

Helpful Language

Throughout the book I'll use a few phrases interchangeably; others that you might be expecting I won't use at all. Here's why: In an effort to see people better, how we talk about and refer to those made in the image and likeness of God is important. Yes, our US policies, and even our Bibles, might use words that are accurate in their context and definition and yet don't help us (in today's context and cultural meaning) refer to people in the most humane ways. If we can talk about our neighbor, whom we are commanded to love as ourselves, in a more dignifying way, we should make every effort to do so.

Alien is a great example of this. While the word is correctly translated in our Bibles and not incorrect in referencing a foreigner or noncitizen, it's also a term that has come to refer to extraterrestrial, nonhuman life and usually carries a negative connotation. The term distances us from the humanity of a person, making it too easy to think of someone as other, or not like us. We have better, more humanizing words we can use instead, like *immigrant, refugee,* or *asylum seeker.* Also, *undocumented immigrant* or *immigrant without status* will always be used here instead of calling someone illegal. Here's why: The *action* a person committed may be illegal, and it will be called such, but I will not refer to a *human being* as illegal. I will always choose the more humanizing terms, and I hope you will too. Today's demands to use the exact right words or labels can be frustrating. I get that. But before you think me oversensitive, all I'm saying is that if we can do better (when talking about fellow image-bearers), we should. Humanizing words and phrases don't dilute the truth; if anything, precise language elevates the truth (of any situation or people group), and much of that is helped by using people-first language.

Since many words in the immigration conversation have

become muddled, their meaning changing based on who is using them, it's best for us to be on the same page up front. Here are a few definitions for words I will use:

- *Immigration:* The act of traveling into a country for the purpose of permanent residence there.[1]
- *Emigrate:* To leave one's place of residence or country to live elsewhere.
- *Immigrant:* A person who comes to a country to take up permanent residence.
- *Refugee:* One that flees; a person who flees to a foreign country or power to escape danger or persecution.
- *Asylee/asylum seeker:* Someone who has been granted asylum (safe stay in a foreign country) or who is seeking asylum.[2]
- Ger: The Hebrew word translated in our Bibles as "alien," "foreigner," "immigrant," "stranger," or "sojourner" depending on the translation (I will use these interchangeably).

Deconstructing versus Detangling

Here's one more thing I want to clarify right away: talking about this subject matter doesn't mean we're deconstructing our faith. I'm often told that my involvement in conversations about human dignity—especially immigration—is a "slippery slope" to extreme liberal policies or unorthodox, progressive theology, that wading into these waters is a dangerous drift from a conservative perspective and way of thinking. Maybe you've heard this too. From the outside looking in, I can see how my journey might look like deconstruction or something like it. But contrary to what some people might think, looking carefully at this conversation from a biblical perspective doesn't mean you've lost your anchor or that you're taking a sledgehammer to your faith. This isn't a smash-and-grab job. It's a thoughtful examination, an intentional surgery that may require painful resetting of structures and perspectives we've relied on for far too long. After engaging the topic of immigration more closely, I love Jesus more than ever, and I'm still orthodox in my interpretation of the Scriptures. I've been told I'm "a little too passionate" about some of these issues. But I'm okay with that. You can be too. We can be passionate about people and their flourishing; Jesus certainly was.

Bottom line, we're not deconstructing here in these pages, we're *detangling*.

Detangling is a careful kind of work, slow and steady. We're sorting out the long, strong thread of our faith from all the other things that have gotten bunched up together. Too many things have been attached to Jesus that don't belong. Too many contradictions have killed the faith of so many, and they can take years to unwind. Too many voices of people who look and sound just like us have been our only influence in this space. We can do better. That's why at the end of each chapter we'll hear stories from people who have done life and ministry with immigrant populations or are immigrants themselves. There will also be reflection and discussion questions so you can start this journey privately or with your friends, asking good questions along the way.

Be encouraged: this journey gets us to a good place—one that honors God and those he's created. At the beginning, we may feel unsure of stepping out onto this ledge, but eventually, we'll feel our hair blowing unobstructed in the wind, and it will feel great. The newfound viewpoint will be worth it. Life is hard. The world is full of pain. But Jesus is not afraid of our questions, tears, and rants. So let's ask what truly furthers his kingdom and detangle it from our own. This is a holy pursuit, and we'll be better for it.

But where do we start? This is a vastly complicated subject. The answer might seem too simple, but for the Christian, we always look to Jesus first, remembering that it was his welcome toward us that changed everything. Everything about our lives is and should be different because of the welcome he extended to us. He didn't start with our sin or our shortcomings. He didn't invite the thieves and tax collectors to dinner to demand they quit their way of life. All our new ways of living eventually came about from one simple approach: welcome. It doesn't mean the other details don't matter; it simply means that Christlike welcome changes things. It changes what we say, how we think, and who we deem worthy of our compassion.

Welcome one another as Christ has welcomed you, for the glory of God. (Rom. 15:7)

If Christ started with welcome, as his followers, let's start there too. I can do this. You can do this. We should do this together.

Let's go.

how did I get here?

On a hot afternoon in southern Mexico, two thousand miles from home and in a fenced-in courtyard full of kids, I stood next to two young girls, listening as they told a story I found difficult to comprehend. It isn't like me to be speechless. It isn't like me to retreat. But my head started spinning and my confident countenance shifted into an unsettling fog.

I needed a moment, somewhere out of sight and away from the conversation.

Smiling, I excused myself from the group. Wandering down a cement hallway, I pushed open the first door I saw and slipped inside an old storage room.

Alone inside that musty, stuffy closet, I broke down.

I buried my face in my hands, and my body doubled over as I gave in to uncontrollable sobs. I cried and cried as these words raced through my head: *How could I have missed this?*

The Invitation I Didn't See Coming

My personal passions and career paths have always revolved around pro-life advocacy. But when we adopted our second child, I stepped back from my much-loved role as director of sanctity of human life at Focus on the Family to make space for my own family. That's when I received an interesting invitation. America's newsfeeds were (and always seem to be) full of stories of "migrant caravans," "invasions at the border," and "unaccompanied minors," so World Relief—a global Christian humanitarian organization I had partnered with in the past—was taking an immersion trip to Oaxaca, Mexico. They would listen to local city and church leaders talk about the realities of immigration, explore the cultural dynamics of the region, and visit shelters housing families and unaccompanied migrant children.

"I think you should come and invite some of your friends," Michelle, the trip host, announced confidently during our initial meeting. "Think anyone else you know would be interested?"

I paused at the question. My life, work, and education all took place in conservative evangelical circles. Who *would* come with me? The conversations happening around immigration and the opportunity to join in intrigued me, but I wasn't sure who else would feel the same. Even asking felt risky.

But as an Enneagram Eight, I am not afraid of hard conversations, so it was impossible for me not to try.

This was back in 2017, when the rhetoric around immigration and asylum seekers was intense. The plight and care of refugees—a topic conservative Christians had passionately advocated for and acted on for decades—was becoming "too political." My evangelical community started distancing themselves from this once-uncontroversial people group. You may remember fiery rhetoric about the border wall, increased security spending, ending DACA (Deferred Action for Childhood Arrivals), and outlawing sanctuary cities. I scrolled through my long list of friends and colleagues thinking, "Who wants to get into all of this?"

For me, being a Christian and being pro-life have always gone hand in hand. As I understood it, the sanctity and dignity of every human life weren't in question; they were a banner under which *all* followers of Jesus fell in line. I had grown up in the church as a happily devoted pastor's kid, learning about God's love and compassion long before I could articulate such things. Like many in the evangelical culture, I only heard *pro-life* defined in the traditional sense, as "against the practice of abortion." But as an adult, I started working professionally in pro-life spaces and was mentored into an expanded definition that took my pro-life commitments beyond the preborn and adoption space.

As a lifelong Christian, I thought this expanded definition made perfect sense. In my advocacy work, I leaned hard into a holistic definition of what it meant to be pro-life, creating resources and content to help others speak up for preborn children as well as other vulnerable populations across the full spectrum of life. After decades of searching for my calling, *I had found it.* This holistic pro-life definition and approach lodged in my soul. Recognizing vulnerable people became my passion. Inspiring and equipping the church to move closer to them became my purpose. Being holistically pro-life challenged me, fed my desire to keep learning, and pulled me into fascinating statistics and stories from around the globe. My curiosity about other people, their work, their lives, and their viewpoints only increased as I learned. I could feel my world growing bigger—my world *and* my faith. While some friends and family suggested I was moving too far away from my home base, I never felt an urge to leave the conservative Christian theological ballpark, so to speak. I simply wanted to start running *all* the bases. I felt called to inspire the church to genuinely and tangibly recognize the *imago Dei*, the image of God, in every person.

In all this I thought my definition of pro-life was robust and deep. In reality, I had just been skimming the surface. That's when I received the call from World Relief inviting me on a trip south of the US border.

Eager to kick up some dust in my own heart and run full

speed into what God had next, I agreed. I spent weeks mentally preparing myself, knowing full well it would be an emotionally hard trip. But no amount of prep work could have prepared me for the seismic shift God was about to make in my heart. I would not come home the same.

Four Days in Mexico

For four days our guides walked us through the streets of Oaxaca, Mexico. The weather was dry and hot, but the culture and landscapes enamored us as we moved from one educational experience to the next. We sat with government officials and nonprofits, with pastors and shelter directors, learning about regional migration and US immigration dynamics from their perspective.

Sitting inside a family migrant shelter in Oaxaca, Mexico.
A shelter guest painted this mural about their journey
migrating through Mexico to the United States.

One afternoon we toured a shelter for unaccompanied migrant children. The center was government-run, set up to care for children from southern parts of the continent who were lost, deserted, or separated from their parents during the journey north. As we neared the shelter, our guide prepped us with initial information. As we pulled up to the building, soberness hung in the air as we peered out the windows. My mind was swimming with questions—and, if I'm honest, with anger and judgment too.

What sort of person leaves their child behind?
What kind of mother could do such a thing?

I couldn't help but think of my own babies at home. I could never, *ever* abandon my children to seek a better life for myself. I don't even let my children cross the street without their hands in mine, much less cross a country or a continent on their own.

As we shuffled through security, children of all ages came into view. We were encouraged to greet and play with them for a while, then took a short tour of the center. That's how I met Maria and Alicia.[1] Maria, thirteen years old, walked toward us with an eight-month-old baby on her hip. Alicia was a babe herself, at eleven years old, yet she too carried a baby in her arms, a newborn only eight days old.

My friend Heather and I smiled at the two young girls, so close to the ages of our own children back home. We told them they were beautiful, as were the babies they carried. We asked what country they were from and whose babies they were watching. Since we didn't speak their language, we held their gaze and our smiles as the shelter staff and translator explained what neither Heather nor I were prepared to hear: Maria and Alicia were neither babysitters nor big sisters: *they were the mamas.*

These kids were mothers? I was utterly undone. I immediately started thinking about my own daughter back home.

What if this were *her* life? These girls, these babies who had had just given birth, were nursing infants without their own mothers to teach or protect them. One thing was clear: no child chooses this, to be a mother at age eleven or thirteen.

My body froze while my mind started spinning, trying to find a slot, a file folder of experience or context that could help me make sense of it all. Nothing fit. Nothing was adequate to make sense of this horror that had happened to them. I became increasingly, desperately curious to understand why these girls were in this situation: preteen mothers, separated from their own mothers, in a government-run shelter far from their homes and families. I began to ask questions, more and more questions. And I started to question myself too. Why had I not been aware of these situations before?

In all my work creating whole-life pro-life content, I had been unaware that this reality was horrifyingly common for migrant women and their children. I learned that women who leave their homes (frequently from one of the "Northern Triangle" countries of El Salvador, Guatemala, and Honduras) to trek north through Mexico toward the United States experience violence, sexually abuse, or assault along the way. Yet the reality of staying home is even more terrifying. These women and girls flee intense violence in their communities. Femicide—the murder of women and girls—rates in the Northern Triangle are among the highest in the world. Even at home, women and girls are profoundly unsafe. Children must cross gang territory to attend school, a task so dangerous that many drop out and can't complete their education. Violence is everywhere. The cartels claim every block and business that flourishes, taxing those that show any sign of financial stability. Local gangs force young boys to kill or be killed. Husbands and fathers despair of being able to support their families given the economic realities, much less keep them safe.[2]

As we stood in front of these two girls, I could hear the

laughter of other children their age playing games with other women from our group. Without more to ask, say, or share, I stepped away. My anger turned into a strange haze. I needed a minute. I ended up weeping in the storage closet.

I wept so loudly that one of our trip hosts rushed in to see what had happened. "Bri, oh my goodness, are you okay?" Cathleen asked.

I couldn't answer her. My throat was swollen with sobs. Cathleen was visibly concerned as she wrapped her arm around me. And then, quite abruptly, I heard, "She's all right."

I quickly turned, surprised by the statement. It was Michelle, the woman who initially invited me on this trip. She was completely unphased by my distress. So much so that it startled me. She wasn't being insolent; she simply had experience. Michelle had been here before. "She's all right, Cathleen. She's just grieving what she's missed."

Michelle signaled for Cathleen to leave the room. "Let's give her a minute."

Michelle had named it. I wasn't confused or even angry, really. I was grieved. Grieved that the American church had missed the realities and cries of migrants so badly. Not only had we missed these things we'd also busied ourselves making excuses, biblically shrouded justifications for our well-versed indifference. "We can't take everyone." "They should just come here legally." "People need to stand up and fix their own governments." "God made borders for a reason." "Safe and secure borders first." While each of these statements can be right and true in a certain context, in the realities of real migrants, they just didn't hold irrefutable status any longer. How could they? Things were vastly more complicated.

In that moment, in the corner of the storage closet, I became convinced: if my friends could see what I just saw, they would be just as grieved as I was.

I was sure of it.

On my first trip across the border, this is the storage closet where I processed what I had just heard at an unaccompanied child migrant center in Oaxaca, Mexico.

The rest of our time in Oaxaca was deeply meaningful and life-changing. We learned from nonprofits and cultural museums, walked city and market streets, met with Mexican government officials and migration offices, toured shelters, and heard from migrating families. My eyes were opened, and my life could not—would not—be the same.

When I returned home, *normal* felt like an insult. My life felt like a slap in the face to the pain I had seen and heard. Yet what could I do? My community already knew exactly what it thought and felt about immigrants and refugees. Who would want to hear my story? Who wants to be challenged on the issues of immigration? Literally no one I knew. But I couldn't unsee what I had seen.

I was convinced that more people needed to know more about the realities our neighbors beyond the border were facing—so convinced that my career took a new path. Fast-forward five years, and I'm the director of an immigrant advocacy project (Women of Welcome) working with groups like World Relief (the humanitarian arm of the National Association of Evangelicals) and the National Immigration Forum.

When I started in this work, I thought *seeing* these situations or even hearing these stories was the silver bullet solution to create change.

Goodness, I had so much to learn.

What is Women of Welcome? Watch here.

Overlooking one of the border crossing bridges on one of my first trips to El Paso, Texas, and Ciudad Juárez, Mexico.

A Conversation I Didn't Expect

You know those dinner parties where you don't know anyone but have to make small talk? The ones where you have to keep smiling and asking others about their lives to fill the time while the ice melts in whatever drink you're holding? I'm an enthusiastic extrovert, but I've never been one for small talk, and these days, awkward, read-the-name-tag social situations are precarious for me. By the time someone asks, "So Bri, what do you do for work?" I've already evaluated the risk of sharing what I *actually* do.

Do I offer the easy, palatable "I'm an advocate for refugees"? Or do I take a chance and tell them the whole truth? "I direct a nonpartisan advocacy project for immigrants and refugees that helps Christians think about immigration issues from a biblical perspective rather than a political one."

Fun way to start a conversation, right? After my answer, I always smile and wait. The response could go either way, and it's fun to watch the wheels turn behind their eyes. I usually have three solid seconds to sip my drink before I hear the verdict. For some, my work is interesting and commendable. Others start scanning the room for a friend to save them.

I wonder if the Lord chuckles a bit when he puts me in these situations. I'm sure it's amusing to watch me go from, "I love your dress!" to "Well, I think we can have safe borders *and* humane policies for the immigrants and refugees who come to our borders."

In every online or in-person conversation with my conservative Christian community about the work I do, I'm aware of the objections they may have. It's like there's a news ticker in the lower third of my brain, continuously running with alerts as I dialogue: *Warning! You just said we should welcome immigrants. This translates to, "You're for open borders." Address this before it gets too messy.*

Or *Mayday! Mayday! You just mentioned asylum seekers coming through the southern border. Immediately pivot to the US's thorough vetting process. Quick!*

For some, talking about immigration makes for sweaty palms and waves of anxiety. But for me, I've found a secret that seems to work. Immigration is a tricky subject; no one is ever 100 percent knowledgeable about *everything*. (I mean, they have lawyers for this stuff.) But I have a trustworthy tool that helps me confidently have the conversation—any conversation, really.

Listening.

That's the secret: listening wed to deep empathy for the other person's viewpoint no matter how opposite it may be from mine. I certainly don't do this perfectly, but I'm forced to work at it every single day. And while listening sounds too simple for such a big problem, it's actually quite hard when you're passionate about something. But what's most difficult is this: for listening to be effective, our motivation must be genuine. Real listening is *not* something we can (or should) fake. Listening as a means to an end does not work. People can sense we don't really mean it.

God first taught me this lesson as I sat front and center in a boardroom in Washington, DC. It still makes me emotional to recall the scene.

A few months after I took the job as director of Women of Welcome, people who had long advocated in the immigration space started asking, "Wait, there's a project engaging evangelicals *for* immigrants and refugees?"[3] At the request of the National Immigration Forum (a nonpartisan advocacy group), I was invited to speak to influential leaders about the work I believed could engage and reengage evangelical Christian women around the topic of immigration. I shared—to a room of mostly unbelievers—my belief that the true heart of my evangelical community was *compassion* for people. Confidence to fuel their compassion and speak up was what they lacked. And since many of us don't have proximity to the daily realities of immigrants or refugees, we have developed a blind spot. I told these leaders that immigration fit squarely within my holistic pro-life world-view and that I was confident other women could and would make this connection too. I shared how visiting migrants across the border changed my life and confessed the deep grief I felt for missing the deepest layers of the conversation.

I'm pretty sure I cried a little.

Then the floor was opened for questions. The first raised hand didn't offer a question but a comment, and I could tell she spoke with restraint. Kelly represented a foundation few conservatives would have likely worked for or associated with. She had a small frame, beautiful skin, and blonde hair; it was easy to smile and meet her eyes.

When called upon, she offered a memorable pause. The room became quiet. She leaned forward in her chair and looked straight at me. As she held my gaze, I felt my smile fade. I sensed this wasn't going to be a pat-on-the-back comment, so I looked right back into her eyes, giving her my full attention. Then, with a deeply serious and concerned expression, she said, "I'm not going to give up my views on abortion."

That was it. That's all she said, and the room stayed silent, as if everyone felt the calculated concern she had just named.

Honestly, I was a bit surprised. But mostly just deeply sad. I wasn't sad that she was pro-choice. No, what struck me as I watched her quivering chin pronounce those words was the grief I felt over the distance she assumed existed between us. Here she sat, listening to a rookie immigrant advocate talk about the "true heart" of evangelical women "who love people well." I had raised her hopes that evangelicals would share her heart for vulnerable immigrants and refugees, but the second I mentioned our pro-life convictions, her heart sank. She believed us to be at an impasse, one she could not and would not cross.

This was a courageous thing for her to say across the room, and I admired her for it. Tension hung in the air after she spoke.

That's when the Holy Spirit created some space.

Leaning forward in my chair, as gently and sincerely as I could, I replied, "I didn't expect that you would."

We both took a deep breath. I think everyone in the room took a breath, but I wasn't looking anywhere else. I wanted to hold her gaze. I wanted her to know I heard her. Saw her. Felt the pain she restrained. I wanted her to *see* that knowing all this didn't make me angry and that I wasn't intimated. I remember thinking, "Is that what she heard me say? Is that what she thinks I'm asking of her?"

This would-be impasse made me want to get closer, hear more.

Yes, I had *seen* a few things, even seen her in that moment. But to do any good, I needed to *listen*. Even to those I disagreed with. It's the only way we'll relearn how to work together as fellow humans and image-bearers of God. Kelly* and I certainly don't agree on everything. I'm not going to recalibrate my convictions on abortion (and neither is she) to make progress in the immigration space. And yet here we are.

Kelly leaned back in her chair and crossed her arms. "You're telling me evangelical women would work with me on immigration even if I don't give up my views on abortion? I don't know anyone like that."

I smiled back at her. "Yeah you do. Me."

How Did I Get Here?

So how did I get I get here? To this calling of listening and advocacy? The only way to explain it is *God*. I didn't pick this space. I didn't seek it out. I took a phone call and said yes to an invitation—Jesus took it from there.

People ask me if I get bombarded with criticism for advocating on behalf of immigrants and refugees. The truth is, yes, I do. From all sides. This is a lonely place to be. But I'm clear on my role, and that gives me confidence to remain steadfast. It's quite simple: It's not my job to force you to believe what I do. Not in this book, online, or even at a coffee shop. I have only one agenda, and it's *not* to get you from point A to point Z. It's simply not to leave you where you are.

So consider this *your* invitation to get close to something that makes you uncomfortable. If along the way you find yourself alone, grieving in a closet about what you've missed or wondering how you got tangled up in a conversation about pro-life issues and immigration, you're in good company. You're not alone.

It's good to ask yourself how you got here. *Here* is a good place to be.

Nicole's story

I've been an immigrant twice, and I've served with an organization that worked in relief and development amid one of the largest refugee crises of our time. I've helped bring aid to those who fled. I listened to and wrote stories so that donors would hopefully continue to help. I stood looking over the vast rolling hills of the world's largest refugee camp and thought I knew something about the vulnerability of a transitory life. I knew *nothing*.

When I started listening, really listening, I realized how one-sided my knowledge was of why people leave and why people need sanctuary. For years, I volunteered in refugee resettlement in the US and then with the Rohingya camps in

Bangladesh. I was sitting in the living room of a Bangladeshi friend when I realized I had closed my eyes to the realities of immigration, the obstacles to entering the US or other places that offer safety, and the ways we make it harder for those already in peril.

I knew my friend's daughter went to college in the US and asked about her offhandedly. My friend's eyes turned red, and she looked away. She hadn't seen her daughter since she left for college and didn't know when or if she would see her again. Because of their work with the church, their lives had been repeatedly threatened. When her daughter went to the US on a student visa, she claimed and was granted asylum. She could stay because she had proved she feared for her life if she returned. Since that time, though, immigration rules had changed, and her family couldn't get visas to visit her.

I saw the pain of a mother separated from her daughter, maybe forever. Yet she chose to do what was best for her child. I didn't dare ask about her teenage son in the other room and what the future held for him.

That was a turning point for me, and I started listening more intently to what was happening inside our own (US) borders. What were the laws that granted asylum? Who were we keeping out and why? This was about the same time caravans of migrants started showing up at our southern borders, and then news erupted of family separation. The divide between two parties widened to what seemed like an abyss impossible to cross. The threats of walls seemed like an insurmountable barrier to climb.

I detest the name-calling, finger-pointing news reporting of our day. All it does is perpetuate more hate in a world that is dying without love. I can hardly stomach watching it anymore. Yet I won't look away. Vulnerable people were right in front of me for years, and I still didn't see it. How many of us are turning away because this subject doesn't reach our front doorstep or because we can't care about one more issue?[4]

Discussion Questions

1. Who or what influences you most on matters of immigration? (Media, friends, family, the Bible?)
2. What voices in your life are silent on these issues?
3. How do the stories in this chapter connect with you personally? Have you had up-close experiences with immigrants or refugees? What do you know about the US immigration system?
4. What questions do you have as you go forward in this journey?

CHAPTER 2

is immigration a pro-life issue?

In 2018, during the height of President Trump's zero-tolerance policy, I listened to a young woman tell her story of arriving at the border with her children. "We are without a voice, without a body," she explained. "Back home *and* here. But I was coming for protection, to flee violence."

She was a young migrant mother describing her treatment at a US detention facility. She was talking about her immigration experience, but I couldn't help but think of the parallels to abortion. The language and even the phrasing she used were similar. She was without a voice, she was treated and talked about as if she weren't human, and she wanted to escape violence. It sounded like the very thing I would say about a preborn child in any kind of abortion conversation.

As obvious as the connection is to me now, at first glance, I know it can be challenging to see how the topics are related. I still remember the first time I was told immigration didn't belong in the pro-life conversation. I was busy writing and curating content for a ministry I worked for. Tasked with creating a thorough pro-life resource guide, my team enlisted dozens of authors and acquired permissions from various outlets. We were determined to give our constituents the best information on pro-life issues from top theologians, well-trained pastors, pro-life professors, doctors, respected advocates, and elected legislators. Nearly three hundred pages later, I submitted all this hard work for editorial review. At this conservative evangelical ministry, all the content needed to meet strict orthodoxy standards and show theological consistency throughout. We'd never created a resource like this before, so we had to get it right. My team had worked hard, and I turned in the manuscript with a smile. I was proud of the months of work we had put in.

A few days later, I was called to the vice president of ortho-doxy's office. "Wow, that was fast," I thought.

As I walked through the executive wing of the building, I had a bounce in my step, anticipating a good review. The department head was someone I respected and admired (still do). Thoughtful, direct, and kind, he was (and is) one of my favorite people to talk to in the building.

When I got to his door, I gave a confident knock.

"Hi, Bri. Come on in. I just wanted to talk about a few things as I've had a chance to briefly skim your work here."

He plopped down the thick stack of paper with a thud. As he flipped through, I could see a good amount of highlighting.

"Well, all these chapters here are fine: abortion, adoption, disabilities and special needs, human trafficking, poverty, and this end-of-life section—all really good. But there are a few chapters we're going to need to take out."

"Oh, okay," I said sheepishly. "Is something wrong with them? Which ones?"

"Well, this one here, and then this one about immigrants and refugees."

I looked up, confused.

"I, um, have permissions for all this content. Is there some-thing I missed? I realize these are relatively small chapters in comparison to the others, but there's not much content out there—at least in the conservative evangelical space—that we can use that would be agreeable and still challenging for our constituents."

"Oh no, Bri, that's not the issue. These chapters just aren't really a fit. We wouldn't talk about these things in a pro-life book. Correct me if I'm wrong, but I believe the purpose of this resource is to be a handbook, a guide for people to reference about being pro-life. You've taken this beyond the abortion issue. And I can see why. So much of it is relevant and good—"

I interrupted. "So those issues like disabilities, human trafficking, and end-of-life care can stay in?"

"Yes, we can talk about those things if you want to, but these other areas, like immigrants and refugees, aren't a fit. We'll need to take that content out completely."

He said it so matter-of-factly.

I responded more thoughtfully in hopes of getting further clarification. "Okay. I guess I don't understand. Isn't it odd not to mention those issues if we're going to talk about all the others?"

"Well, this is where we need to decide what really belongs in this guide. Maybe we just keep it to abortion. I'll continue reviewing, and then we'll circle back. I just wanted to give you a heads-up."

I left his office, head low, feeling extremely disappointed. But his feedback piqued my curiosity, and after a few hours of reflecting, I realized I was a bit angry. I went to my boss, who had given me the project and instructed me to be holistic, showcasing areas of human dignity that connected to the traditional (anti-abortion) pro-life framework. I sat down on her uncomfortable office couch and told her about my meeting.

"I thought this might happen," she said. "What exactly did he say we need to cut?"

I told her about the two or three specific chapters.

"Oh, that's ridiculous!" she said. "What do they want us to do? Ignore half the Bible?"

I shrugged.

"They're pushing back on our scriptural justification for telling people to care about immigrants and refugees?"

I realized then that I had ignited a fire, one I wouldn't be able to control.

"Well, maybe we just can't include it in our pro-life content," I suggested, trying to pull the conversation back from the ledge we were now undoubtedly on.

"No. The problem is that these topics are too controversial for our constituents. You did nothing wrong. This is something we're going to fight for. It's too important. People are dying. These are all *life* issues!"

And with that, she bolted out of her chair and down the hall to defend our work. I wasn't sure what she was about to burn down, but whatever it was, I wouldn't be the one calling 9-1-1!

After several weeks and rounds of meetings, I was allowed to leave a small minority of content about immigrants and refugees in the book—so small that it was easy to skip over. These chapters I needed to pare down were robust with immigrant stories, testimonies, and experiences. Most of that content ended up on the cutting-room floor. And while some content was allowed to stay (biblical references and theological perspective pieces), from that season on, I knew there was much more to learn, much more to say, many more connections we could have made.

Piecing Together the Puzzle

The truth is, many of us who feel compassion for immigrants and refugees are trying to figure out where our welcome and advocacy for this particular population fits within our traditional pro-life worldview. By calling immigration a "pro-life" issue, are we watering down the term *pro-life* or expanding it too far beyond its common definition in relation to abortion? Are we trying to force a puzzle piece where it doesn't fit? Let me assure you: it fits.

Let's back up for a moment and start at the root of our pro-life convictions. The first question we need to ask ourselves is, "What does it mean to be pro-life?" How do we define that exactly?

Most of us who have been in and around the pro-life movement for years know that there's the traditional definition of what it means to be pro-life, and then there's the more holistic definition. Traditional pro-lifers tend to operate within and define their scope of advocacy around only the abortion issue. Those who subscribe to a broader definition define their scope of advocacy around a plethora of human dignity issues that includes but isn't limited to the preborn.

Webster's dictionary defines *pro-life* as "opposed to abortion." But for Christians, our opposition to abortion is not anchored in or inspired by any dictionary definition or political platform but in our biblical belief about the dignity and sanctity of every human life. Genesis 1:27 says that God created humankind in his own image. We take this verse seriously in preborn advocacy. But this verse also serves as the foundation for defining the sacredness of all human life, from conception to death. These words from the Bible aren't meant to live in a box and be taken out only to defend one group of people.

In Matthew 22:34–39 (my paraphrase), the Pharisees are looking to test Jesus. They ask him, "Teacher, what is the greatest commandment in the law?" Jesus replies, "Love the Lord your God with all your heart, with all your soul, and with all your mind. And the second is this, to love your neighbor as yourself." As followers of Jesus, we are to love God and love others, and every human being, born and unborn, is in this "others" category. "Being pro-life, then, can mean looking at each human being in a way that sees beyond their culture, class, race, ability, age, and opinion, knowing that all of us have equal value and importance to God."[1]

When we think about each and every person, born and unborn, as a unique image-bearer—when we choose to see them as God does—our care and concern for the vulnerable starts to expand. The borders around our definition of what it means to fight for life drifts outward in holistic and holy ways. Our passion for the flourishing of our neighbors becomes more consistent and cohesive. It feels a bit messy at first, but it makes sense. Life and its right to flourish are a continuum, womb to tomb.

A Biblical Definition of Pro-life

If we move beyond a dictionary definition of what it means to be pro-life and instead look at the whole of Scripture to inform our worldview, what do we find? We may be surprised to discover that passages which long anchored us in conversations about abortion also anchor us in other areas of human dignity. I promise this isn't a drift from theologically orthodox ways of thinking. We're simply giving Scripture the room to breathe beyond what we've traditionally given it oxygen to address.

Take a minute to read through these verses that form the bedrock of advocacy for the unborn (this is not an exhaustive list, but it gives us a good start):

- Genesis 1:27—God created man in his own image, in the image of God he created him; male and female he created them.
- Exodus 20:13—You shall not murder.
- Exodus 23:7—Do not kill the innocent and righteous.
- Psalm 100:3—Know that the LORD, he is God! It is he who made us, and we are his; we are his people, and the sheep of his pasture.

- Psalm 119:73—Your hands have made and fashioned me.
- Psalm 127:3–5—Behold, children are a heritage from the LORD, the fruit of the womb a reward. Like arrows in the hand of a warrior are the children of one's youth. Blessed is the man who fills his quiver with them!
- Psalm 139:13–16—You formed my inward parts; you knitted me together in my mother's womb. I praise you, for I am fearfully and wonderfully made. Wonderful are your works; my soul knows it very well. My frame was not hidden from you, when I was being made in secret, intricately woven in the depths of the earth. Your eyes saw my unformed substance; in your book were written, every one of them, the days that were formed for me, when as yet there was none of them.
- Proverbs 31:8 (NIV)—Speak up for those who can't speak for themselves, for the rights of all who are destitute.
- Proverbs 24:11—Rescue those who are being taken away to death; hold back those who are stumbling to the slaughter.
- Jeremiah 1:5 (NIrV)—Before I formed you in your mother's body I chose you. Before you were born I set you apart to serve me. I appointed you to be a prophet to the nations.

We typically use these verses to support our prioritization of and advocacy for the unborn. Yet they also remind us of our "why"—how purposeful and precious *every* human life is. Every person is created to reflect something about God's likeness into the world. Every person (preborn and born) has immeasurable value and worth and is bestowed with an intended purpose. Everyone we see is an image-bearer and therefore should be treated as such.

In the Old Testament, we see an abundance of passages that consistently elevate four specific populations of people. I first encountered the idea of the "quartet of the vulnerable" in the writings of pastor and theologian Tim Keller,[2] which he borrowed from Nicholas Wolterstorff: the orphan, the widow, the sojourner, and the poor.

> This is what the LORD Almighty said: "Administer true justice; show mercy and compassion to one another. Do not oppress the widow or the fatherless, the foreigner or the poor." (Zech. 7:9–10 NIV)

If anyone is prioritized in God's eyes, apparently it's these people. God mandates that his people care for these groups that are uniquely vulnerable, creating laws to secure protection and provision for them among the community.

Every Life Matters

In the New Testament, Jesus engages with a wide number of human dignity issues: people who are outcast, homeless, poor, in prison, or mentally ill. Jesus connects these people together by telling his followers that *everyone* is our neighbor and we are to love our neighbor as ourselves. He levels the playing field by telling crowds that *every life matters*. Throughout his teachings, Jesus brings attention to those who have been pushed outside of cultural rules, religious traditions, and personal preferences. He advocates for the livelihood of those he encounters. Matthew recorded Jesus's specificity on this:

> When the Son of Man comes in his glory . . . the King will say to those on his right, "Come, you who are blessed by my Father. . . . For I was hungry and you gave me food, I was thirsty and you gave me drink, I was a stranger and you welcomed me, I was naked and you clothed me, I was sick and you visited me, I was in prison and you came to me." Then the righteous will answer him, saying, "Lord, when did we see you hungry and

feed you, or thirsty and give you drink? And when did we see you a stranger and welcome you, or naked and clothe you? And when did we see you sick or in prison and visit you?" And the King will answer them, "Truly, I say to you, as you did it to one of the least of these my brothers, you did it to me."

Then he will say to those on his left, "Depart from me, you cursed, into the eternal fire prepared for the devil and his angels. For I was hungry and you gave me no food, I was thirsty and you gave me no drink, I was a stranger and you did not welcome me, naked and you did not clothe me, sick and in prison and you did not visit me. . . . Truly, I say to you, as you did not do it to one of the least of these, you did not do it to me." And these will go away into eternal punishment, but the righteous into eternal life. (Matt. 25:31, 34–43, 45–46)

Without Jesus's holistic engagement and consistent advocacy, many of his image-bearers would have died alone and without hope. They would have remained cast aside (as the culture had instructed) and forgotten by those who had more privilege and power. Jesus's advocacy for these people was shocking. But his followers were told to get close, to become proximate to people and their pain. They were to look for the vulnerable and give of their time. They were to invite to the table those who had never been invited or included. Once at the table, they were given a voice and an unhurried audience with God himself.

From Womb to Tomb

Considering the whole of Scripture, we're hard-pressed to find justification for singling out and elevating one vulnerable population over another. If we're operating from a biblical definition (instead of a dictionary definition) of what it means to be pro-life, then we should prioritize what God cares about. We should hold fast to a more comprehensive conviction about the dignity and sanctity of human life. We should advocate for the heartbeat of the child in the womb, the heartbeat of the child waiting in foster care or in an orphanage, and the heartbeat of the child approaching our southern border. We should advocate for the marginalized in our local communities and for those dying from preventable diseases and starvation in developing nations. We should speak up for the integration of citizens returning to our communities from prison and for the dignified treatment of those in nursing homes and mental healthcare facilities. We should fight for those manipulated and trapped in human trafficking while also seeing the beauty of those who live with disabilities. We should attune our ears, recalibrate our hearts, and use our voices for the flourishing of all our neighbors, just as Jesus did.

For Christians, a *holistic* ethos helps define our values and shepherds our priorities. It keeps us consistent in our various efforts to protect the dignity and sanctity of *all* life—from womb to tomb.

The Web We Weave

In the (traditional) pro-life movement, there is often concern that those who subscribe to a more holistic definition don't use their voices to advocate for preborn children and instead elevate other vulnerable populations. I can tell you, holistic pro-lifers have a similar concern toward the traditional crowd, fearing that preborn children have long been elevated above everyone else and little advocacy is being done for those already born. The reality is that both concerns are valid. We can all do a better job adhering to the *whole of Scripture* to advocate for the *whole of life*. This isn't a competition to see who fails the least or the most; it's an invitation to learn more about God's vision for life and how we can step into it. There is much common ground between us, and we'll miss out on an even bigger life-movement if we remain at odds.

When we wade into the margins, where vulnerable people usually find themselves, we see how interconnected these life issues really are. Unfortunately, many people outside the church readily see these connections and wonder why many pro-lifers remain inconsistent or silent about issues beyond abortion. The world not only has seen us leave various populations of people largely unaddressed and uncared for but also has often watched professed Christians adamantly advocate *against* the provisions that could sustain the livelihood of the vulnerable (more on that in a minute). It's confusing to hear Christians say they care deeply about family values and innocent life and yet seem numb to the pain points of life outside the womb. Life issues aren't simplistic and linear, they're a web.

As the world watches Christians rally around the abortion issue, it hears us claim we're pro-woman. And while I can attest that the movement *really is* pro-woman (I know this from my former work with nearly two thousand pregnancy centers and medical clinics around the country), there is a limit to what the vast majority of these centers can do to help vulnerable women and their families flourish past the toddler years. Don't get me wrong; these centers are doing hard, heroic, and holy work. These workers remain steady at the front lines of the abortion issue, loving vulnerable women and their babies, as they have been for decades. But when pro-lifers downplay or defund many of the public programs that support vulnerable new families, the lack of tangible support becomes glaringly obvious. Since 1973 (the year abortion was legalized), conservative legislators have had the opportunity to expand and support child tax credits, parental and childcare benefits, and affordable healthcare and to create paid family leave among other family support programs.

Yet these are the very kinds of programs and policies that have historically been the first on our legislative chopping block. To the watching world, this seems inconsistent with family values and true concern for women postbirth.

Now that *Roe v. Wade* is overturned and thousands more women will carry their babies to term, the need for these programs is even greater. I'm grateful some people are having much needed, long overdue discussions about expanded support systems for women. This is where our commitment to human dignity must move beyond just the preborn. Many young women who choose life, carry to term, and decide to parent find themselves unprepared and unsupported financially, relationally, and educationally. They experience a major gap in tangible support, making them and their children vulnerable during the most formative (and arguably the most stressful) years of parenting and child development.

Many of these vulnerabilities can and do lead to children being placed in the US foster care system. And while the church has traditionally encouraged adoption, much of its response has centered on "easier placements." People will wait years to be matched with a domestic (white) infant instead of navigating international adoption agencies or getting "too attached" to kids in foster care who may be reunited with their families or next of kin. The reality is that our foster care system is bursting at the seams, with approximately four hundred thousand kids in the system in any given year.[3] One hundred thousand of these children—one in four—don't have parental rights attached to them and are awaiting forever families. The average child who is eligible and waiting for a family in the US foster care system is eight years old.[4] These children need permanency and lifelong love if they are to have a fighting chance in life.

One hundred thousand kids are waiting to be adopted, and there are about three hundred thousand churches in the United

States. If one family from every third church adopted one of these children, we'd dismantle this backlog and the constant stream of (sometimes valid) criticism the world levies toward our approach to vulnerable pregnant women. Instead, over twenty thousand children age out of the system every year, making their odds for survival and flourishing low. At the age of eighteen, these kids are on their own. Far too many become extremely vulnerable to human trafficking, join the homeless and unemployed population, face mental health challenges alone, experience food insecurity, and have repeated negative encounters with our criminal justice system, many finding jail or prison a frequent home.[5]

Just like that, these babies we've saved from the violence of abortion may be the very same children who now face *new* threats to their flourishing and livelihood.

If we believe in the inherent value and dignity of pre-born children *in* the womb, we must also find our pro-life voice for those *outside* the womb. We'll find this voice and see *this web of interconnectedness more clearly* as we get in closer proximity to people.

Life-and-death realities become apparent when we start serving minority communities or volunteering in prison ministries and mentoring in reentry programs. We find deeper connection points when we humbly show up to learn and serve in disability and mental health communities or when we participate in the prevention and rescue efforts of young adults from trafficking and modern-day slavery. When we sacrificially give to solutions that create affordable housing and rehabilitation programs for the chronically homeless, these issues become personal. When we begin to walk with those who live within food deserts and offer our professional expertise to fill gaps that exist in healthcare inequities, we'll see this web of connectedness grow.

Many of us adoptive parents have seen this web spin into existence firsthand. Because when you get close to adoption work, you begin to see the painful vulnerabilities so many birth families face (domestically and internationally) that connect to issues of homelessness and inequitable healthcare. You become aware of the accessibility hurdles that continue to exist for people with disabilities or mental health challenges. Likewise, when you get close to the criminal justice world, you also come face-to-face with the drug abuse crisis, asylum seekers being held in public and private detention centers, race sentencing biases and education disparities. When you get close to human trafficking realities, you understand how vulnerable children are in our foster care system or refugees and asylum seekers are during their journeys to find safety. This web, this interconnectedness of issues that affect the ability for human life to flourish outside the womb, is nearly endless.

Advocating for life can feel overwhelming and complicated. But being holistic in our pro-life approach and rhetoric isn't a redefinition. It's a recognition—a revival—of long-standing Christian ethics and teaching. For instance, the Catholic Church has been discipling their congregations with a "consistent life ethic" through their Catholic Social Teachings, part of their church doctrine since the mid-nineteenth century. Almost a hundred years ago, a group of Protestant Christians sought to pair their beliefs about God and the Bible (the "fundamentals") with active service and love toward their fellow humans, and the modern evangelical movement was born. All the way back in the earliest days of the Christian faith, a handbook called the Didache instructed first-century Christian communities in how to care for children left alone to die and how to welcome strangers into their homes (to give a few examples) alongside instructions in baptism and communion. So while some might feel this is a new and trendy way of being pro-life, caring for all life *and its flourishing* has always been a foundational part of the Christian faith tradition.

You Can't Do It All

A common concern I hear about this expanded web of life issues is regarding scope: "These other issues are out of scope for us." "This kind of definition, this kind of approach, unfairly demands pro-life advocates and organizations change and add to their program offerings." "It's not what we're called to as an organization." Most people are surprised when I agree. I'm not talking about dismantling ministry-specific mission statements to solve all life issues. Nor am I advocating for organizations to programmatically and logistically operate as whole-life pro-life entities. Pregnancy centers shouldn't take on refugee resettlement or start tackling international food insecurities. I'm not advocating for a programmatic shift for traditional pro-life ministries, but instead a "word and deed" gut check for Christians. We need accountability and consistency in how we see, speak about, and serve others. Being holistically pro-life means we work as one body, the body of Christ. We can't all be an eye, a foot, and a hand—nor should we work to that end. What we need is for every part of the body to work together in order to function as we should.

> The body does not consist of one member but of many. If the foot should say, "Because I am not a hand, I do not belong to the body," that would not make it any less a part of the body. And if the ear should say, "Because I am not an eye, I do not belong to the body," that would not make it any less a part of the body. If the whole body were an eye, where would be the sense of hearing? If the whole body were an ear, where would be the sense of smell? . . . If all were a single member, where would the body be? As it is, there are many parts, yet one body.
>
> The eye cannot say to the hand, "I have no need of you," nor again the head to the feet, "I have no need of you." . . . But God has so composed the body . . . that there may be no

division in the body, but that the members may have the same care for one another. If one member suffers, all suffer together; if one member is honored, all rejoice together.

Now you are the body of Christ and individually members of it. (1 Cor. 12:14–17, 19–21, 24–27)

My passion doesn't need to be your passion or vice versa. God designed and intended each of us to have unique experiences, giftings, and purposes. Each of us is equipped to be the hands and feet of Jesus right where we are called.

But to be a healthy, functioning body, we must be aware of what else is happening in the body. We need to be aware of each other's needs and pain points. This allows us to pray with deeper wisdom, share resources more effectively, and advocate with consistency.

Thinking about life holistically makes us aware of what it really takes to save a life.

Remember the pro-life resource book my team worked on? Another way of putting this is that you, your local church, or your organization can't possibly tackle every chapter in that book. You can't be an expert on everything. But we need every chapter to be included *in the book* to give us the full picture and create unity in the body of Christ.

Do you feel called to save babies and women from the pain and violence of abortion? Go for it. Do you feel passionate about rescuing people from slave labor and sex trafficking? Do it. Do you want to visit nursing homes each week to love the elderly? I'm cheering you on. Are you determined to reduce the number of kids waiting in foster care or the number of children who go to sleep hungry at night? I couldn't be clapping more loudly. Do you want to make sure those with disabilities aren't forgotten and have more dignified pathways to participate in society? Yes, we need you! Do you want to welcome refugees into American communities? Let's go.

It's not organizational, programmatic, or logistical scope expansion that whole-lifers want to recalibrate. *It's the rhetoric and prioritization of single issues in the public square that we want the evangelical community to be more cohesive and consistent on—together.* Those who speak up against the injustice of abortion and human trafficking shouldn't be silent on the injustice of healthcare disparities that exist across the country. Those who speak up for children languishing in international orphanages or the US foster care system shouldn't be silent on the lack of humane treatment toward children in US immigrant detention facilities. Those who speak out against racial injustice shouldn't be silent about the violence and trauma abortion inflicts on vulnerable women and preborn children. The list goes on. These are *all* life issues. Our organizations and our ministries aren't made to speak to every issue.

But the church is.

You and I must speak up together as one cohesive body of believers claiming that all life is valuable and that our compassion is not political but prophetic. When we do this, we aren't bestowing dignity to others, we're affirming it.

Pro-life Policy

For those who are new to this holistic pro-life definition, let me be the first to reassure you that this does not require you to agree with every public policy or legislation proposed as a solution to these issues. You needn't subscribe to extreme policies and agendas (such as unconditional welfare or open borders, to name a few). It simply means you're committed to applying the whole of Scripture in your advocacy for life issues. You're not expected to be an expert in all these areas, just a consistent, compassionate voice. If we are to love our neighbors as ourselves, how does that affect the way we show up and advocate for others?

My entire life, I had been intuitively taught to believe that how you voted indicated how "pro-life" you were. And yet what I've come to learn is that being pro-life doesn't simply mean voting a certain way every four years. Being *holistically* pro-life has everything to do with the years in between. Yes, we must vote our convictions. But we must also know that our vote will be imperfect. (My friend Eugene Cho taught me this through his brilliant book *Thou Shalt Not Be a Jerk: A Christian's Guide to Engaging Politics*.) Neither party encompasses a perfect platform of programs and policies. I'm not suggesting (in the slightest!) that we minimize the importance of the preborn. On the contrary! But to truly revere the lives of the preborn, we must revere the lives of those already born—and this undoubtedly includes immigrants and refugees.

A few months back I was invited to join a quarterly denominational call with a host of pastors to explain my work with Women of Welcome. When I connected the immigration issue to the pro-life movement, several hands went up. One by one pastors told me, "This makes sense. It takes the politics out completely. A whole-life pro-life approach is what we need." One pastor who was serving an underserved urban area jumped in.

I think what's hard for my community is the inconsistency: Christians just advocating for the preborn. The pain of abortion is real, and yet so are the stomach pains of a child who goes hungry every morning and night. Suffering is real inside and outside the womb. We fought for these babies to live, but in some ways, we have traded one pain for another. I realize (elective) abortion is intentional pain and hunger is not, but why do we not speak with the same passion about both areas of pain?

He was right. Why would we advocate for the right of a child to live, yet not equally advocate for the very things a child needs to stay alive? While we're justifying our indifference to these "after birth" resources (clean water, nutritious food, medicine, healthcare), children die preventable deaths. Our advocacy for sustaining life outside the womb is simply a continuation of our (traditional) pro-life convictions. As Christ's followers, we should speak up consistently, fighting for the dignity and sanctity of *all* lives.

When I started advocating as a whole-life pro-lifer, specifically on the issues of immigrants and refugees, an unbeliever approached me after a talk I gave: "I don't understand you Christians. You fight for a child's heartbeat in the womb, but not for the child's heartbeat at the border. Can you explain that to me?"

I didn't have a good answer.

The world is hungry for a consistent Christian ethic.

It's time for the church to take the lead.

Mary's story

When we started foster care, we began with a week of respite care for a seventeen-year-old from Guatemala and her young daughter. She taught me how to make cantaloupe agua fresca. Then in August 2021, we welcomed Ali, from Afghanistan.

I feel deeply burdened by the crowds of children who desperately need someone to let them in—to simply give them shelter, food, respect, and a place to belong for a season. The stories of how these youth fled their homes and came to the US always shock people, and how wonderful these youth are impresses people. But these youth and their stories are not unusual! There are thousands upon thousands of unaccompanied youth just like them, waiting to be given a chance, waiting for someone with a spare bed to say, "Come on in."

People sometimes think being a foster parent is somehow amazing or radical. It's not. I still go to work, and my husband and I still go on dates. We just live our lives, allowing a child in need to live with us. For anything we may have sacrificed along the way (which is not much), we have gained a hundred times over in blessings from these youth. I wish I could make people understand that they are a blessing, not a burden, but I think that's something you learn only after you get close to them. Proximity changes everything. But because so few people sign up to become foster families , I sometimes feel lonely not being able to share and process my experiences with others. I long to see foster care normalized, especially in the church.

As a foster family we've been able to welcome children from all over the world. Just a few months after our Congolese daughter arrived in the US, she was part of a summer camp where foster youth expressed themselves through art. In their final performance, she wrote and performed a powerful song about God's faithfulness to her as she was abducted by rebel soldiers and separated from her family, eventually escaped captivity, and ran to a foreign country by herself—at age thirteen. I basically held my breath through the whole performance. Afterward, the camp directors told us how she was a leader in that year's cohort—the other foster youth gravitated toward her, and she radiated light. Just a few months ago, our Ali was selected from among his graduating class as demonstrating "outstanding leadership."

These were some of the world's most vulnerable people —defenseless children seeking refuge in a foreign country— and they're overcoming all kinds of obstacles and ascending to leadership among their peers. How is that not the power of God? The Scriptures consistently describe God as the defender of the weak and fatherless. He loves them fiercely! I've had a front-row seat to this love, and it's powerful. You will see this fierce love when you get close to the weak and fatherless. I have watched God provide for our foster youth, surrounding them with good people, opening doors for them to flourish, and nourishing them. I am watching him work in their hearts and strengthen their faith. It is amazing to witness.[6]

With two of my best friends, Kelly Rosati and Elizabeth Graham, at the Evangelicals for Life Conference in Washington, DC. For several years, the three of us, along with Dr. Russell Moore, Phillip Betancourt, an amazing team at Focus on the Family, and ERLC, created these pro-life conferences in an effort to unite and move forward the holistic narrative and biblical worldview of being pro-life for the whole-life.

Our first Evangelicals for Life conference in Washington, DC, where we intentionally invited evangelicals to march alongside others in the predominantly Catholic March for Life event. Pictured here with Elizabeth Graham (now CEO of Stand for Life).

Filming interviews and marching in the March for Life event in Washington, DC, alongside colleagues Jim Daly (President of Focus on the Family), Robyn Chambers, and Tim Geoglein (former Bush staff turned Focus on the Family executive and Washington representative, 2017).

Immigration and pre-born issues intentionally being addressed in the space at the Evangelicals for Life Conference (pictured here with Jenny Yang, senior vice president of advocacy at World Relief at the time, 2019).

Discussion Questions

1. How would you define being pro-life?
2. What role has the pro-life movement played in your life, faith, or identity?
3. Would you consider immigration a pro-life issue? Why or why not?
4. What questions or concerns do you have after reading this chapter?

what does the bible say about immigrants?

One of my favorite childhood memories is playing Sword Drills with my Sunday school classmates. We held Bibles above our heads while the teacher announced a verse reference. The second we heard the last number, we slammed our Bibles down on the table and raced against each other to find the passage. Whoever started reading the correct verse out loud first won a point.

Sometimes someone got it wrong, loudly and assuredly reading John 3:17 instead of *James* 3:17. A quick pause would hover over the room, everyone watching the teacher to see if the reading was correct. If the teacher answered "Nope!", we were back to tearing through the pages.

I loved everything about this game. I loved knowing where to find things in the Bible. I loved not needing to consult the table of contents to find obscure little books like Obadiah and Philemon. It was a competition, and I never wanted to lose. But knowing the Bible wasn't just a Sunday morning drill. Throughout my childhood, the Bible was always in front of me, open on a table and talked about over dinner. Theological discussions were common during cookouts with friends and family. Every home I visited had multiple Bibles on its bookshelves and coffee tables, family heirlooms passed down from great-grandmas and grandpas. After college I left home to attend Dallas Theological Seminary, earning my master's in biblical and theological studies. But even with all my Sword Drill wins, even with all my exposure to God's Word, it was only a few years ago that when someone asked, "What does the Bible say about immigration?" I didn't have much to say. I couldn't answer and didn't have a quick reference to turn to. Turns out, I'm not alone. According to a 2022 Lifeway Research study, most (self-identified) evangelicals find themselves in the same boat I was in. When thinking about immigration,

- Only 21 percent of evangelicals say they are most influenced by the Bible (this stat trails behind media influences).
- Only 30 percent of evangelicals say they have been encouraged by their church to reach out to immigrants in their community.
- Less than 50 percent of evangelicals say that the number of recent immigrants to the US provides an opportunity to show love and introduce them to Christ.
- Yet 76 percent of evangelicals report that they would value hearing a sermon that taught how to apply biblical principles to issues of immigration.[1]

I asked a pastor I loved and respected how he would answer the question. His reply: "The Bible talks about caring for the foreigner, but it doesn't talk about immigration specifically. That's really a political issue."

A political issue. Yeah, that's what I thought too. And though immigration is certainly a political issue, it's also a biblical one. The public policies we create affect people, and every person affected is made in God's image. Every person is someone God loves deeply. As God's followers, we are to care how human beings are seen, treated, and talked about.

Our present-day personal, social, and cultural issues are not lost on God. In his Word, God provides a framework for how to think about people and approach the situations we find ourselves in. What the Bible says about our neighbors should take precedent over any media take or political platform, for as Christians, the Bible is our leading authority on the treatment of people.

Here are two questions for you to consider:
1. What has primarily shaped your views on immigration: partisan politics or Scripture?
2. Do you desire to see this issue more clearly, through the lens of your faith?

It's a challenge to look up from our culture's daily noise and diligently look to the Scriptures for direction, especially if that direction will push against our feelings—and our friends' beliefs and opinions. But hasn't that always been the case for Jesus's followers? Now that I'm involved more deeply in immigrant advocacy work, I've started reading Bible stories I've known since childhood with different eyes. These days, when someone starts loudly and assuredly spouting Scripture to prove a point about immigration, I'm still head-down, looking through the pages myself. I'm on a journey to understand where God is on this. I want to get it right. Want to join me on this journey?

The Quartet of the Vulnerable

Turns out, the Bible doesn't specifically reference immigration policy, just as it doesn't prescribe specific solutions for other modern social conundrums (like abortion, homelessness, hunger, or healthcare challenges). It doesn't say anything specific about modern American policy, I'll give you that. But what about the people our immigration policies effect? Whew, there we have some ground to cover. God has a great deal to say about immigrants and refugees.

If you've taken a class on how to study the Bible, something your professor or pastor may have taught you is that if a word or phrase is repeated in the Bible, pay attention; go back and read it again. Repetition means something is important.

In the Old Testament, the Hebrew word *ger* is repeated often. Translated into English, *ger* appears in our Bibles as "alien," "foreigner," "immigrant," "stranger," or "sojourner." Appearing over ninety times in the original Hebrew, its frequency in various stories and commands to the Israelites gives us a solid framework for understanding God's heart for immigrants.

Often *ger* is mentioned in conjunction with three other groups of people: the orphan, the widow, and the poor. Theologian and divinity school professor Nicholas Wolterstorff calls this grouping "the quartet of the vulnerable."[2] When laying out his instructions for how the Israelites should live with and among others, God continually elevates this grouping of vulnerable people above all. *Pay attention*, God says. *Take care of them. Be vigilant in bringing justice to their circumstances.*

The First Movement of God's People

Migration is an ongoing theme in Scripture. God is always calling his people to *go*: go to new places and live among new people. Sometimes it's for their safety, sometimes for survival, sometimes simply because God wants to bless them, to give them good things to help their families flourish. Other times, people are exiled, forced from home because of their own sin or the trouble caused by evil nations. But one way or another, from Genesis to Revelation, the Bible is full of migration stories.

Genesis 1:26–27 explains why God cares so much about human beings: we're made in God's image. We individually reflect and collectively represent something about God himself. Right here in our creation story, we're reminded that immigrants and refugees are image-bearers, endowed with inherent dignity and value. After God created humankind in his image, he blessed them and said, "Be fruitful and increase in number; fill the earth and subdue it. Rule over the fish in the sea and the birds in the sky and over every living creature that moves on the ground" (Gen. 1:28 NIV).

God made us with a desire to work and to live life to the fullest. We are designed to be creators, stewards, contributors, and cultivators. We have God-given potential to do incredible things, no matter where we're born, what language we speak, or what culture we are raised in. Everything about this truth is beautiful and good.

It's when Adam and Eve must leave the garden that things get complicated. After disobeying God, their move from Eden was the first migration: they were forced to leave and never come back. They could no longer stay where they wished to live, and life was no longer black and white. We haven't stopped migrating since.

The next major story of migration is when God tells Abram in Genesis 12:1–3,

> Go from your country and your kindred and your father's house to the land that I will show you. I will make of you a great nation, and I will bless you and make your name great, so that you will be a blessing. I will bless those who bless you, and him who dishonors you I will curse, and in you all the families of the earth shall be blessed.

So Abram and Sarai moved. They migrated to the promised land, and then they migrated back out of the promised land and into Egypt. Fear and hunger motivated their immigration to Egypt, and when they arrived, Abram lied about his marriage status to receive better treatment from the Egyptian officials. They found themselves uniquely vulnerable in this new territory.

As is clear in these stories, much of migration in the Bible was hard, as it continues to be today.

God's Concern and God's Commands

God's people continually shuffled around the region of Canaan, sometimes by choice, other times by force. Joseph involuntarily migrated to Egypt after being sold into slavery by his brothers (Gen. 37:18–36). After rising in status and earning favor in the eyes of Pharoah, Joseph became a global leader, his people given land and place. But they soon became too numerous and prosperous for the Egyptians' comfort, who enslaved them once more. After four hundred years of slavery, God raised up Moses to lead a mass migration out of Egypt (Ex. 12:31–33).

After this exodus, God reminded his people to pay attention to those coming in and out of their communities. Let's take a look at his instructions:

- **He wanted his people to be mindful of the *ger* in their midst, so he instructed the people to provide for them.**

    When you reap the harvest of your land, you shall not reap your field right up to its edge, nor shall you gather the gleanings after your harvest. You shall leave them for the poor and for the sojourner: I am the LORD your God. (Lev. 23:22)

    When you gather the grapes of your vineyard, you shall not strip it afterward. It shall be for the sojourner, the fatherless, and the widow. You shall remember that you were a slave in the land of Egypt; therefore I command you to do this. (Deut. 24:21–22)

You shall divide this land among you according to the tribes of Israel. You shall allot it as an inheritance for yourselves and for the sojourners who reside among you and have had children among you. They shall be to you as native-born children of Israel. With you they shall be allotted an inheritance among the tribes of Israel. In whatever tribe the sojourner resides, there you shall assign him his inheritance, declares the Lord GOD. (Ezek. 47:21–23)

- **He calls his people to protect the *ger* among them and to give them rest.**

   The seventh day is a Sabbath to the LORD your God. On it you shall not do any work, you, or your son, or your daughter, your male servant, or your female servant, or your livestock, or the sojourner who is within your gates. (Ex. 20:10)

   You shall not oppress a hired worker who is poor and needy, whether he is one of your brothers or one of the sojourners who are in your land within your towns. You shall give him his wages on the same day, before the sun sets (for he is poor and counts on it), lest he cry against you to the LORD, and you be guilty of sin. (Deut. 24:14–15)

- **He instructs his people to be generous and hospitable toward the *ger*, treating them like family.**

   The LORD your God is God of gods and Lord of lords, the great, the mighty, and the awesome God, who is not partial and takes no bribe. He executes justice for the fatherless and the widow, and loves the sojourner, giving him food and clothing. Love the sojourner, therefore, for you were sojourners in the land of Egypt. (Deut. 10:17–19)

When a stranger sojourns with you in your land, you shall not do him wrong. You shall treat the stranger who sojourns with you as the native among you, and you shall love him as yourself, for you were strangers in the land of Egypt: I am the LORD your God. (Lev. 19:33–34)

- **The Lord wanted his people to take him seriously on these matters; he issued warnings if they failed to heed his instructions.**

   You shall not wrong a sojourner or oppress him, for you were sojourners in the land of Egypt. You shall not mistreat any widow or fatherless child. If you do mistreat them, and they cry out to me, I will surely hear their cry, and my wrath will burn, and I will kill you with the sword, and your wives shall become widows and your children fatherless. (Ex. 22:21–24)

Clearly, God was serious about how he expected his people to treat the *ger* among them. He even promised to side with the immigrants over his own people if they didn't provide for and protect the most vulnerable in their communities!

God's People Far from Home

Not only does God love immigrants—men, women, and children whom he created and cares for—but he knew the Israelites would themselves end up in lands far from home, needing the same kind of mercy and care from others.

Daniel, one of the beloved characters in the Bible, was forced to migrate to Babylon when King Nebuchadnezzar besieged Jerusalem (Dan. 1). While living in Babylon, he and Shadrach, Meshach, and Abednego were servants in a kingdom that had leveled their homeland. They maintained their culture and heritage the only way they could: by differentiating what they ate and what they believed. Eventually it was their unwavering faith and their presence in this foreign land that proved to the entire kingdom that the God of Israel was the only god worth worshiping.

Ruth was a foreigner who married an Israelite. After her husband's untimely death, she followed her mother-in-law, Naomi, into the land of Judah, intentionally staying in Bethlehem during the barley harvest (Ruth 1). Naomi knew her people had a system in place to care for widows and migrants; they survived by gleaning the fields after the initial reaping. This practice was a dedicated allowance for sojourners, commanded by God for the survival of those who found themselves in vulnerable situations. Ruth's migration made her an immigrant in the land. In marrying Boaz, she unknowingly became the great-grandmother of Israel's greatest king, David.

In the Psalms we read, "The LORD watches over the sojourners; he upholds the widow and the fatherless, but the way of the wicked he brings to ruin" (Ps. 146:9). Many times David sought refuge and asylum in enemy territory to escape King Saul (1 Sam. 19, 21–23). Without a safe place to go, he became desperate. At times David was so desperate that he resorted to acting mentally ill; other times he begged enemy leaders for a covering over his family so they would survive.

The Prophets

The primary vocation of the prophets was to bring God's words to the people, applying God's laws to current events.

Their messages consistently echoed God's heart for justice and mercy concerning the vulnerable and oppressed. Here are a few poignant passages:

> "Thus says the LORD of hosts, Render true judgments, show kindness and mercy to one another, do not oppress the widow, the fatherless, the sojourner, or the poor, and let none of you devise evil against another in your heart." But they refused to pay attend and turned a stubborn shoulder and stopped their ears that they might not hear. They made their hearts diamond-hard lest they should hear the law and the words that the LORD of hosts had sent by his Spirit through the former prophets. Therefore great anger came from the LORD of hosts. "As I called, and they would not hear, so they called, and I would not hear," says the LORD of hosts, "and I scattered them with a whirlwind among all the nations that they had not known. Thus the land they left was desolate, so that no one went to and fro, and the pleasant land was made desolate." (Zech. 7:9–14)

> Thus says the LORD: Do justice and righteousness, and deliver from the hand of the oppressor him who has been robbed. And do no wrong or violence to the resident alien, the fatherless, and the widow, nor shed innocent blood in this place. . . . But if you will not obey these words, I swear by myself, declares the LORD that this house shall become a desolation. (Jer. 22:3, 5)

> Then I will draw near to you for judgment. I will be a swift witness against the sorcerers, against the adulterers, against those who swear falsely, against those who oppress the hired worker in his wages, the widow and the fatherless, against those who thrush aside the sojourner, and do not fear me, says the LORD of hosts. (Mal. 3:5)

One of the most overlooked yet sobering stories about God's wrath on those who disregarded the plight of sojourners and refugees is in Obadiah. The Hebrew name Obadiah means "servant of the Lord." Yet the nation of Edom was a servant to none but themselves. Their priorities and lifestyle were only for their own flourishing:

> The pride of your heart has deceived you,
>> you who live in the clefts of the rock,
>> in your lofty dwelling,
> who say in your heart,
>> "Who will bring me down to the ground?"
> Though you soar aloft like the eagle,
>> though your nest is set among the stars,
>> from there I will bring you down,
> declares the LORD. (Obad. vv. 3–4)

Why was God so angry with the Edomites? As the descendants of Jacob's brother Esau and a direct neighbor to Israel, they were in position to help when Babylon invaded Jerusalem. Instead of coming to their aid, they "stood aloof" and took advantage of their neighbors' misfortune. God fiercely rebuked them for this lack of engagement, saying,

> Because of the violence done to your brother Jacob,
>> shame shall cover you,
>> and you shall be cut off forever.
> On the day that you stood aloof,
>> on the day that strangers carried off his wealth
> and foreigners entered his gates
>> and cast lots for Jerusalem,
>> you were like one of them. . . .
> Do not stand at the crossroads

to cut off his fugitives;
do not hand over his survivors
    in the day of distress.
For the day of the LORD is near upon all the nations.
As you have done, it shall be done to you;
    your deeds shall return on your own head.
        (Obad. vv. 10–11, 14–15)

The first time I thoroughly reread Obadiah, I had just visited a crowded tent camp in Mexico. My immediate thought was, "Lord, are we in the United States the modern-day Edomites?" We, too, see vulnerable migrants at our borders with nowhere else to turn and remain silent while legal pathways become fewer and more cumbersome. What would the Lord say to us today?

The Incarnation

The most notable emigrant of the New Testament is Jesus. Some suggest his coming to earth was a celestial migration of sorts, as he chose to come from heaven to live on earth among us. Jesus and his earthly parents (Mary and Joseph) can also be described as refugees to Egypt, asylum seekers fleeing the wrath of King Herod's edict to kill every Jewish boy under the age of two.

From the moment Jesus came to earth, he and his family were vulnerable. They traveled in the cover of darkness across cities and regions. They most assuredly relied on the mercy of strangers. They directly benefited from God's laws requiring kindness, generosity, and hospitality to sojourners. They likely stayed in strangers' homes and walked through pastures they didn't own as Mary and Joseph prayed and waited on God's direction for the right place to raise their son.

Jesus's movement didn't stop once Herod was dead. His

ministry was that of a migrant, traveling from place to place preaching the love of God with "no place to lay his head" (Matt. 8:20 NIV).

A Love That Levels the Playing Field

While the Old Testament elevates the quartet of the vulnerable (orphan, widow, sojourner, and poor), Jesus raises the bar substantially in the New Testament. He levels the playing field by including *every person in society*.

If this weren't challenging enough, in Matthew 25:31–46, as you'll recall from the previous chapter, Jesus declares that one day we'll all be identified, sorted out, *known* by our actions toward the vulnerable: "Truly, I say to you, as you did not do it to one of the least of these, you did not do it to me."

I imagine the disciples' blank stares. *Jesus, how on earth could we possibly see all this? Do all this?* It's a valid question, especially if you take your eternal future seriously. Any one individual cannot singlehandedly take on the world's pain. I'm thankful for the reminder God gave Samuel: "The LORD sees not as man sees: man looks on the outward appearance, but the LORD looks on the heart" (1 Sam. 16:7).

Remember when Jesus was preaching near the sea of Galilee and people throughout the region would *not* stop coming to see him?

> When Jesus heard this, he withdrew from there in a boat to a desolate place by himself. But when the crowds heard it, they followed him on foot from the towns. When he went ashore he saw a great crowd, *and he had compassion on them* and healed their sick. Now when it was evening, the disciples came to him and said, "This is a desolate place, and the day is now over; *send the crowds away to go into the*

villages and buy food for themselves." But Jesus said, "They need not go away; you give them something to eat." They said to him, "We have only five loaves here and two fish." And he said, "Bring them here to me." Then he ordered the crowds to sit down on the grass, and taking the five loaves and the two fish, he looked up to heaven and said a blessing. Then he broke the loaves and gave them to the disciples, and the disciples gave them to the crowds. And they all ate and were satisfied. And they took up twelve baskets full of the broken pieces left over. And those who ate were about five thousand men, besides women and children. (Matt. 14:13–21, emphases mine)

For many Americans, when we see crowds of migrants coming to our southern border, we're inclined to simply say, "*No más.*" But if our gut reaction, the thing driving our next move, isn't compassion, we need to reread this story. Just the sight of the large crowd *moved* Jesus to compassion. Not fear, not eye-rolling or hand-wringing (although that's likely what the disciples were doing). Jesus told them not to send anyone away but to feed them. "With what?" they demanded.

Can you imagine Jesus at that moment? Here he is, God incarnate, and the people who believe him to be the Messiah are standing before him exasperated about not having enough resources to do *what he asked them to do!* I can see Jesus looking straight up to the heavens, taking a deep breath, and saying, "Lord, please give me patience . . . Guys, bring me what you have. Let me show you what it looks like to trust me with *everything.*"

No, Jesus doesn't leave us alone to do this work. He does it with us. Jesus doesn't ask us to love our neighbors because it's the right thing to do. He asks us to help bring people to himself.

WHAT ABOUT ROMANS 13?

One of the most common conversations surrounding immigration is around the rule of law, as outlined in Romans 13.

> Let every person be subject to the governing authorities. For there is no authority except from God, and those that exist have been instituted by God. Therefore whoever resists the authorities resists what God has appointed, and those who resist will incur judgment. (Rom. 13:1–2)

How do we apply these verses well?

My friend, and editor in chief for *Christianity Today*, Russell Moore helps explain in a conversation we had together here:

What do we do with Romans 13?

Compassion and Action

So far in this chapter, we've taken a second look at the Bible, paging through, finding passages we had forgotten. Here's the question: Are we seeing our own situation clearly? Are we seeing migrants and our country's immigration challenges *first* through the lens of our faith? Are we getting this right—or do we need to go back to flipping pages?

During my most recent trip to Juárez, Mexico, with Women of Welcome, we visited a shelter I'd never been to before. Usually, we stay close to the border, but this shelter was forty miles away, deeper into the city. As we pulled up to the curb, our driver and host offered a few words of introduction: "We're at a shelter for young mothers and their children. They've never had American visitors before. Your group will be the first."

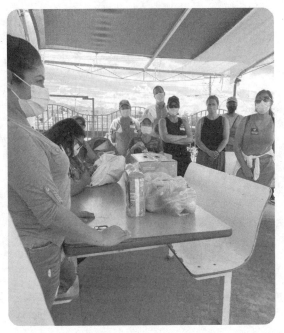

Women of Welcome immersion trip participants listening to shelter staff outside maternity shelter in Ciudad Juárez, Mexico.

Talk about a humbling moment. As we filed out of the hot and stuffy van, we walked through steel pronged gates and sat down at an old picnic table under the partial shade of a worn tarp. The fence was locked behind us. As we listened to the shelter director, I could hear a mix of joy and anxiety in her voice. This was new for them too. But she wanted us to meet these mothers. She wanted us to hear their hearts and see their faces.

The women welcomed us, showing through simple hospitality just how much we had to learn. After breaking the ice by playing Mexican bingo and water balloon games with the kids, we sat down for a time of mutual listening and sharing.

Women of Welcome trip to Ciudad Juárez, Mexico, to visit families in migrant shelters. Our group is praying over shelter coordinator, Maria.

As we stood in a circle hand in hand, offering prayer requests and blessings, one young pregnant mother (who couldn't have been more than twenty-five) spoke. She started with her head up, looking at us all, and said, "It's nice to be with you." Then her head dropped, and she looked at the floor. Letting go of her neighbors' hands, she wiped the tears from her eyes.

"I'm so sorry I stepped on your territory. But my life . . . I had to for my kids. I'm so sorry."

A flood of emotion swallowed the room as she leaned into the shoulder of the woman next to her and sobbed.

Throughout my years of work in immigration, I've read hundreds of migrants' stories. Through Women of Welcome's educational immersion trips, I've had the privilege of hearing some of these stories firsthand. The shame migrants feel for leaving, for coming, for crossing, for being caught, for living in shelters is immense. Every part of their journey is layered with feelings of shame and unworthiness. I had read and heard about this shame, but I had never *seen* it.

No human being should have to apologize for trying to save their children. No human being should feel ashamed for trying to survive. It was a bottomless moment of sorrow, and we had nothing to offer but our solidarity and tears.

As I've taken a fresh look through the Bible, I'm the one who feels ashamed. Why have we not provided for the travelers in our midst as God so frequently and passionately commanded? Why have we not prioritized their needs over our own as the prophets and Jesus asked?

Church, are we getting this right?

Are we seeing the hungry, the thirsty, the homeless, the sick, and the stranger?

Do we remember the words of the law, of the prophets, of Jesus and at least *try* to follow God's commands? Or are we standing aloof, allowing the collapse of legal pathways for those we should welcome?

I know what you may be thinking, because my mind goes there too: Not everyone coming here is a single mother looking for safety. And you're right. Not everyone is. (We'll dive into that in the chapters to come.) But for the hundreds of thousands of women, children, and families looking for hope at our southern border, if we look first through the lens of our faith, scouring through our Bibles for the answers, what do we find?

When Jesus saw the crowds, he was moved to compassion; and his compassion moved him to action. Is your compassion moving you anywhere? Is it moving you closer to the vulnerable, or are you finding yourself stuck, isolated, and comfortable where you are? It's important to wrestle with these questions because we constantly need to recalibrate our hearts and our lives toward the vulnerable, because Jesus commanded his followers to do so.

For centuries Christians have been moving across the globe to fulfill the Great Commission: "Go therefore and makes disciples of all nations, baptizing them in the name of the Father and of the Son and of the Holy Spirit, teaching them to observe all that I have commanded you. And behold, I am with you always, to the end of the age" (Matt. 28:19–20).

Hundreds of thousands of people from around the world are approaching our borders. Do we see this as a divine moment to bring our loaves and fish? Do we see this as an opportunity to fulfill the church's Great Commission? Or do we ask our leaders and lawmakers to push people away to fend for themselves?

Helping serve lunch with other shelter staff and visitors in Ciudad Juárez, Mexico.

Checking Our Biases

Some of us think we're doing fairly well—maybe better than most—at caring for those who are poor, a single mom, a child in foster care. When a lawyer approached God in the book of Luke, he likely felt the same way. The text tells us he was looking to test Jesus and felt justified in his current approach to life and standard of loving others. Translation: "Jesus, could you be more specific? Who around here do you want me to love? Not all of them are my neighbors."

> But he, desiring to justify himself, said to Jesus, "And who is my neighbor?" Jesus replied, "A man was going down from Jerusalem to Jericho, and he fell among robbers, who stripped him and beat him and departed, leaving him half dead. Now by chance a priest was going down that road, and when he saw him he passed by on the other side. So likewise a Levite, when he came to the place and saw him, passed by on the other side. But a Samaritan, as he journeyed, came to where he was, and when he saw him, he had compassion. He went to him and bound up his wounds, pouring on oil and wine. Then he set him on his own animal and brought him to an inn and took care of him. And the next day he took out two denarii and gave them to the innkeeper, saying, 'Take care of him, and whatever more you spend, I will repay you when I come back.' Which of these three, do you think, proved to be a neighbor to the man who fell among the robbers?" He said, "The one who showed him mercy." And Jesus said to him, "You go, and do likewise." (Luke 10:29–37)

For those of us familiar with this exchange, we know how shocking this story is. Many biblical commentators and scholars suggest that no respectable Jewish person mingled with

Samaritans. They were of mixed heritage and considered unworthy of equal respect or kind regard. Some commentators suggest that Jewish people went to great lengths to avoid Samaritans in the region, adding up to four days to their journey when traveling from Judea to Galilee. Centuries of begrudging and hating the existence of Samaritans was their way of life. Then Jesus humbled all who listened by making an "undeserving" Samaritan the hero of the story.

What were the disciples thinking when Jesus answered as he did? Degrading Samaria was a cultural norm handed down for centuries. I think Americans can get caught in this same mentality. We say disparaging things about Mexico, the Northern Triangle, or other countries to the south. We make generalizations about and look down on other ways of life, other cultures. "They've messed up their country. We don't want those kinds of people coming here." We've heard family or friends say these things for years, haven't we? Without even knowing it, we end up dismissing the humanity of a whole region, entire countries and cultures, without meeting a single person who resides there.

This is a dangerous place for our hearts. Jesus knows this. He knows our hearts full well. It's no wonder he takes all whom we despise and calls them our neighbors.

A New Question

Sometimes we think the Bible insufficient to address "the way the world is now." But if the words of the New Testament and the ministry of Jesus don't encompass where we are in society today (with new nations, borders, government order), then we insult God and show ourselves inconsistent in applying other Scriptures about Christ's life to our present circumstances. Yes, the world looked very different when Jesus walked the earth.

But as Christians, we know the Bible is alive and active, still cutting through bone and marrow, testing the depths of our hearts. Treatment of people, especially vulnerable people, was and still is a priority for Jesus. As his followers, we need to get this right.

So the question shifts from "What does the Bible say?" to "What do our hearts want to hear? What do our eyes want to see?" The question becomes "Will we (the American church) choose to see this issue through the lens of our faith and let our faith inform our attitudes and actions?" I fear we've become vastly more comfortable putting on the shades of whatever partisan platform or pundit we ascribe to, memorizing those talking points instead of God's talking points.

The Scriptures have always been a part of my life, and I *still* missed it.

So let's take a fresh look. There's no gimmick or game here, just a curiosity to see what we've missed. This time we're not flipping through pages and finding Bible passages to win points—this isn't a competition. Our goal has *nothing* to do with pride and *everything* to do with people, so we'll talk about people first. Make yourself some coffee, and let's dig in together.

Nori's story

Nori came to the US from Venezuela with her parents when she was four. She was a young teen before she realized they didn't have the proper documentation and the future she'd imagined for herself was in jeopardy. The DACA program gave her hope again. As a Dreamer for the last eight years, she's been able to study and work.

Her status wasn't something she talked about with her

friends though. "I was terrified of what people would think of me." She would spend hours volunteering, wanting people to see her as good, because then if they found out about her status, maybe the good would overpower the "bad."

As she got older, she realized she couldn't keep quiet about having come to the country as an undocumented child. "Keeping these fears and concerns to myself tormented me. I felt like I was living a double life." Nori says she realized she wanted the people around her to know her fully. "The girl sitting next to them in Sunday school was the person they thought was a threat," she says. "Knowing me and knowing the truth, hopefully, would soften their hearts and make them see something different."

"I think especially from a Christian perspective we must remember Christ himself was this child," she says. "He also had to leave to go to Egypt so that he wouldn't be killed as a young child." Her family came by plane. She imagines those today trekking through the desert exposed to evils of nature and man to ask for safety in a place they think they will be welcomed, only to realize that won't be the case. "It's heartbreaking. We forget to love the person who is going through this terrible, terrible time."

She is grateful for the experiences she's had because of moving to the US, but twenty years later, she still feels a sense of sadness. There is an entire country and a family she'll never know. Her experience has given her greater empathy for others in similar situations.

She thinks of the response she would like to receive when she tells people her story: "I'm happy you're here." She says she would love people to say that, regardless of her legal status.

Nori says her faith sustains her and that she is encouraged whenever she finds others talking about migrants from a lens of faith. Growing up, she was encouraged by reading the migration narratives in the Bible, and she reminds us to turn to the Bible to remember how to welcome others. "God sometimes needs us to leave the one place we know to walk into the darkness and the dangers," she says. "It's our job to welcome our brothers and sisters who are on that journey."[3]

Discussion Questions

1. What is your relationship to the Bible? Did you grow up reading and studying the Bible, or is the Bible new to you?
2. Did the statistics regarding the degree the Bible influences evangelicals' views on immigration surprise you? Why or why not? Did they line up with your own experience?
3. What stories or teachings from the Bible in this chapter surprised you?
4. What areas of theology or biblical teaching related to immigration would you like to learn more about?

who is welcome here?

In 2020 the United States had more immigrants living in its borders than any other country in the world. Today, more than forty million of us were born in another country, accounting for about one-fifth of the world's migrants. The population of immigrants in the United States is incredibly diverse, with almost every country in the world represented.[1] This isn't surprising; America has been *the* popular destination for economic opportunity and liberty since the nation was founded. For many who have the privileges of finances or family, immigration to the US has been possible.

Yet while we pride ourselves on being a nation of immigrants, we have a history of denying welcome to those we feel are unworthy, too different, or too much of a social burden. Now that we've taken the time to consider what God thinks about immigrants, it's worth asking what *we* think about immigrants.

Without looking at our past, we will have a hard time understanding where we are now or how to move forward, so let's revisit some of our history together.

A Brief History Lesson

In June 1939, the MS *St. Louis* approached the coast of Miami. World War II had not yet begun, but Europe was on the brink.

The groundwork in Nazi Germany was in place, and Jewish citizens were experiencing increased levels of harassment and persecution. As a result, 937 passengers were aboard the *St. Louis*, nearly all of them German Jews hoping to find safety in the United States. Germany was actively pushing Jews to leave the country, but there was little hope for safety elsewhere on the continent. So nearly one thousand humans bravely boarded a ship that would take them to the other side of the world, far from their home and heritage, far from anything they knew—but, they prayed, closer to safety.

Yet they had a major problem: they lacked the legal paperwork that would allow them to disembark in the United States. Still, the world knew they were desperate, so they hoped to be afforded mercy and safe haven.

When they approached North America, the answer was no. Not here, not this time. These image-bearers were turned away by the United States, by Cuba, and by Canada. Unable to find a port of entry in this hemisphere, the ship and her passengers were sent away by immigration authorities.

President Roosevelt had previously considered opening the nation's doors to Jewish refugees but dropped the idea when it proved unpopular. The official telegram from the State Department instructed the passengers to "await their turns on the waiting list and qualify for and obtain immigration visas before they may be admissible into the United States." Canada's stand was similar, citing the problematic number of Jewish refugees who would certainly follow if this first ship was allowed to safely enter Canada.

Most—620 of those aboard—were sent back to Nazi-occupied Europe. Many were interned in concentration camps. Ultimately, 254 men, women, and children died.[2]

Did the United States regret this decision? Yes and no. Yes, in that we changed our policy toward refugees after World

War II, receiving (for a time) more refugees than any other country. Yes, in that the Department of State apologized to the survivors in 2012—generations later.

But no, in that we continue to make similar choices today.

This wasn't the first—or last—time our nation turned a blind eye to those seeking safety. Our country has a sordid history when it comes to welcoming the world, a sordid history when it comes to valuing life. We have a history of needing *and* rejecting those coming to our shores and borders, and this history has influenced the systems, cultures, and communities we have today. Since the 1700s, we've simultaneously welcomed and scorned immigrants. We've metaphorically cemented two conflicting billboards along our border: *Help Wanted* and *Keep Out*.

Questions about who belongs in America were raised as early as the American Revolution. In 1751 Benjamin Franklin wrote the following in response to German immigrants "invading" Pennsylvania: "Why should [immigrants] . . . establish their Language and Manners to the Exclusion of ours? Why should Pennsylvania, founded by the English, become a Colony of *Aliens*, who will shortly be so numerous as to [change] us instead of our Anglifying them, and will never adopt our Language or Customs, any more than they can acquire our Complexion?"[3]

And then some thirty years later George Washington, in a speech to a group of Irish immigrants, said the following: "The bosom of America is open to receive not only the opulent and respectable stranger, but the oppressed and persecuted of all nations and religions, whom we shall welcome to participate to all of our rights and privileges, if by decency and propriety of conduct they appear to merit the employment."[4]

While the following list is certainly not the complete history of immigration in the US, it highlights some of the most influential movements to demonstrate how our nation's political approach has influenced our welcome of others:

- 1751: America's future founding father questions what kind of people belong in the new colonies.
  - Benjamin Franklin refers to German immigrants as invaders of Pennsylvania.
- 1783: The American Revolution ends.
  - George Washington addresses the group of Irish immigrants (with the sentiment quoted on the previous page).
- 1619–1860: The Transatlantic Slave Trade—Approximately 12.5 million Africans are forced to migrate to the Americas over nearly two hundred years. Black image-bearers endure slavery, torture, and horrific abuses, and from 1787 to 1868 are legally considered only three-fifths of a person.
- 1790: The Naturalization Act—Any free white man of "good character" living in the United States for at least two years becomes eligible to apply for citizenship. Without access to citizenship, nonwhite men have no access to basic constitutional protections, including the right to vote or own property.[5]
- 1820–60: The First Wave—Consisting mostly of Irish and German immigrants, the first major migration to the US lasts until the Civil War. They make their way across the ocean because of famine, civil unrest, and lack of economic opportunity.[6] Dissent rises among the initial colonial settlers, and derogatory signs and comic illustrations that negatively stereotype new immigrants are common: "Irish need not apply" signs are posted in storefronts and businesses.
- 1882: The Chinese Exclusion Act—A constant flow of Chinese workers immigrate to America, building railroads and working in gold mines, clothing factories, and agriculture. As Chinese immigrants become successful, anti-Chinese sentiment skyrockets. White workers blame

Chinese immigrants for loss of jobs and low wages, even though they made up only 0.002 percent of the United States population. The Chinese Exclusion Act, which prevents Chinese immigrants from coming to America, is the first in the nation's history to restrict a specific immigrant group.[7]

- 1924: Immigration Act (National Origins Quota Act)—This act closes off nearly all immigration to the US for four decades, with exceptions made for those from the Western Hemisphere. Visas become a requirement for the first time (Germany, Great Britain, and Ireland account for 70 percent of all available visas). Asian, Southern European, and Eastern European immigrants are extremely limited. Illegal immigration increases. The Border Patrol is created to curb illegal crossings along the Canadian and Mexican borderlands.[8]

- 1942: The Bracero Program—This program is created to help fill labor shortages during World War II, allowing Mexican agricultural workers to enter the United States temporarily. The program ends in 1964.[9]

- 1948: The Displaced Persons Act—This temporary bill allows admission of 200,000 refugees from Europe, and asylum seekers already in the United States are allowed to adjust their status.[10]

- 1952: The McCarran-Walter Act—This act ends the exclusion of Asian immigrants.[11]

- 1953: Refugee Relief Act—Also known as the Emergency Migration Act, it intends to provide relief for Southeastern European refugees and orphans who were unable to seek asylum in the US under previous acts.[12]

- 1965: Immigration and Nationality Act—This act re-creates the country's approach to immigration, eliminating national origin, race, or ancestry as basis for legal entry into the US. Instead, priorities are based on family relations and work skills.[13]

- 1960s–80s: Cubans flee Fidel Castro's regime. With heightened anti-communist efforts in play (domestically and abroad), the US assists with the transport and processing of thousands of political asylum seekers.[14]

- 1980: The Refugee Act—The Office of Refugee Resettlement is created to process and assimilate incoming refugees. The formal and legal definition of a refugee is updated to align more succinctly with that of the United Nations, defining a refugee as someone with a well-founded fear of persecution due to their race, religion, nationality, membership of a particular social group, or political opinion.[15] To date (2022) the US has resettled over three million refugees from all over the world.[16]

- 1986: Simpson-Mazzoli Act—Signed by Ronald Reagan, this act grants amnesty to more than three million immigrants living illegally and without permanent status in the US.[17] As of today (2023) this is the last comprehensive immigration *reform bill.*

- 2012: Deferred Action for Childhood Arrivals (DACA)— Created during Barack Obama's administration, DACA provides temporary protection against deportation and allows work status for children brought to the US by parents who crossed the border illegally. Called "Dreamers," this group of approximately 800,000 immigrants lives in limbo as the policy doesn't provide a path to citizenship and requires continual reapplication every couple of years.[18]

As you can see, the United States has not had any meaningful or significant immigration reform in over thirty years. Stalled by the need for Congress to agree on and provide a solution, minor policies and executive orders complicate an already fractured system. As a result, we find our nation frustrated and unequipped to accommodate the continuous flux of immigrants and refugees who continue to arrive at our borders seeking economic opportunity and refuge.

It's Neither Red nor Blue

From the onset of our nation, the attitudes we have held toward others—the ways we see them—have influenced our immigration policies. While some believe one political party to be better on these issues than the other, both Republicans and Democrats have vacillated in their messaging and actions. Here is a *very* brief summary of our most recent administrations and their approaches to immigration:

- Reagan Administration
  - Helpful
    - Passed bipartisan Immigration Reform and Control Act of 1986.
    - Set high refugee resettlement ceilings.
  - Unhelpful:
    - Actively discouraged those fleeing conflicts in the Northern Triangle from applying for asylum relief; pressured asylum seekers to "voluntarily return" rather than pursue their asylum cases.
    - Signed agreement with Haitian dictator Jean-Claude Duvalier to push back any Haitians caught by the coast guard trying to flee to the US.
- George H. W. Bush Administration
  - Helpful:
    - Increased legal immigration avenues with bipartisan Immigration Act of 1990, formally establishing US asylum policies.

- Created Temporary Protected Status for those who can't be returned to home countries due to dangerous conditions.
- Ramped up refugee resettlement numbers.
  o Unhelpful:
    - Allowed the continued denial and horrible treatment of Haitian migrants after a brutal coup on the island (1991) by sending them to overcrowded facilities in Guantanamo Bay before turning them back without any chance to make an asylum claim.
- Clinton Administration
  o Helpful:
    - Passed the Child Citizenship Act of 2000.
    - Passed 245(i), a section of immigration law that allowed immigrants who entered unlawfully to adjust status if they had a US citizen spouse or other family sponsor and paid a financial penalty.
  o Unhelpful:
    - Passed the hard-line Illegal Immigration Reform and Immigrant Responsibility Act of 1996. The bill prevented undocumented immigrants from "getting in line" to access legal status and made the asylum system far more restrictive. (This was widely considered one of the most harmful immigration laws of the past thirty years).
    - Militarized the border and created a strategy called "prevention through deterrence," which pushed desperate migrants into dangerous and isolated desert regions instead of creating legal pathways for people to pursue in their home countries or at legal ports of entry.
    - Continued repatriation of Haitians despite campaigning against it.

- George W. Bush Administration
  - Helpful:
    - Recognized the need for immigration reform and pushed for a bipartisan, comprehensive immigration bill, but failed to pass it.
    - Passed commonsense border security reform.
    - Played a role in rebuilding refugee resettlement after 9/11.
  - Unhelpful:
    - In an effort to modernize the Department of Health and Human Services, US Citizenship and Immigration Services (USCIS) tended to respond with a military approach to humanitarian needs along the southern border.
- Obama Administration
  - Helpful:
    - Recognized the need for immigration reform and pushed for a bipartisan, comprehensive immigration bill; the bill passed the Senate in 2013 but failed in the House.
    - Provided protection to Dreamers through the Deferred Action for Childhood Arrivals (DACA).
    - Continued wall construction where needed at the border, significantly reducing the percentage of "got-aways" at the border (migrants who have crossed illegally, evading apprehension).
  - Unhelpful:
    - Became known for large-scale immigration arrests and deportations, eventually earning the name "Deporter-in-Chief."
    - Failed to properly respond to a sharp rise in unaccompanied children at the border in 2014,

resulting in poor and overcrowded cage-like conditions for children in detention facilities.

- Trump Administration
  - Helpful:
    - Granted Deferred Enforcement Departure for Venezuelans during his last days in office.
  - Unhelpful:
    - Reduced annual refugee intake numbers to historic lows.
    - Severely cut refugee resettlement and other humanitarian immigration pathways, such as asylum. Effectively eliminated the refugee pipeline system, which is still (as of 2023) not fully staffed and rebuilt.
    - Separated thousands of families at the border with the implementation of a "zero-tolerance policy," in most cases failing to keep track of where parents and children were separated and deported to. As of this writing, thousands of families remain separated, as children were kept in the US and parents were deported back to Mexico and Central America.
    - Significantly cut back legal immigration avenues by implementing travel bans, public charge rules, and "extreme vetting."
- Biden Administration
  - Helpful:
    - Increased annual refugee intake numbers.
    - Reissued the acceptance of unaccompanied asylum-seeking children.
    - Increased federal specialized childcare centers to house children in more humane conditions

while awaiting their court proceedings or to be connected with sponsor families.

- Ended travel bans from Muslim-majority countries.
- Created the Family Reunification Task Force, dedicated to reunifying families that were separated during the previous administration.
- Allowed for the resettlement of over seventy-five thousand people from Afghanistan after US withdrawal from the country.
- Allowed for prioritization of processing Ukrainian refugees after Russia's invasion.

o Unhelpful:

- Inability to get Congress to work together on productive bipartisan solutions.
- Lack of sustainable border solutions; maintaining reactive (versus proactive) approach to humanitarian and security needs.
- Kept the refugee resettlement ceiling at the historically low level of fifteen thousand that had been set in 2017.
- Data shows an increase in immigrant detention numbers.
- Continued to keep Trump-era policies (like Title 42 and the "third country" asylum ban) in place along the border, denying asylum seekers and refugees from some South American countries the ability to seek asylum in the US.[19]

It might surprise you, as it did me, that relying on any one party to be more welcoming or better on immigration issues hasn't worked out. Every president has had an agenda. Treating vulnerable people as political pawns to motivate a voting base has proven to work extremely well—not just in immigration but in other human dignity areas like human trafficking and abortion. It's good to be curious and pay attention to the motivations of our elected officials, as these agendas dramatically affect whom we welcome to this country.

Relationship and Rhetoric

It is dangerously easy to motivate Americans by framing or feeding our perceptions of others. Don't believe me?

Let's look at some recent history to see how the media influences public opinion and our country's leadership.

Desperation in the Middle East

In campaign speeches before and after his election, Donald Trump was quite vocal about refugees and immigrants. Here are just a few of his comments:

> I hear we want to take in 200,000 Syrians. And they could be—listen, they could be Isis [Islamic State]. . . . I'm putting the people on notice that are coming here from Syria as part of this mass migration, that if I win, if I win, they're going back.[20]

> When Mexico sends its people, they're not sending their best. . . . They're sending people that have lots of problems, and they're bringing those problems with us. They're bringing drugs. They're bringing crime. They're rapists. And some, I assume, are good people.[21]

> I do business with the Mexican people, but you have people coming through the border that are from all over. And they're

bad. They're really bad. You have people coming in, and I'm not just saying Mexicans, I'm talking about people that are from all over that are killers and rapists and they're coming into this country.[22]

The people of Germany are turning against their leadership as migration is rocking the already tenuous Berlin coalition. Crime in Germany is way up. Big mistake made all over Europe in allowing millions of people in who have so strongly and violently changed their culture![23]

The United States will not be a migrant camp, and it will not be a refugee holding facility—won't be. You look at what's happening in Europe, you look at what's happening in other places, we can't allow that to happen to the United States. Not on my watch.[24]

In meetings across the country and in the White House, Trump was recorded saying,

"We have people coming into the country or trying to come in, we're stopping a lot of them, but we're taking people out of the country. You wouldn't believe how bad these people are. These aren't people. These are animals."[25]

It was reported that after growing frustrated with lawmakers who came to the Oval Office hoping to protect immigrants languishing in developing nations, he asked,

Why are we having all these people from shit hole countries come here? . . . Why do we need more Haitians? Take them out.[26]

Soon after his inauguration in January 2017, President Donald Trump issued a series of executive orders banning people traveling from seven predominantly Muslim countries—Iran, Iraq, Libya, Somalia, Sudan, Syria, and Yemen—also suspending the resettlement of all Syrian refugees.[27] Americans had mixed feelings on this. The headlines either criticized the new move as blatant bias and·discrimination or defended it, citing that more thorough vetting processes were needed for countries prone to breed and export Islamic terrorism. Political conservatives favored the president's travel bans, as fears about Sharia law and radical, unwanted culture change in America continued to be the rhetoric that resonated with the right-wing base.

While security experts from previous administrations flooded news outlets, affirming that current vetting processes were strong and sufficient, thousands of families found themselves in limbo after the bans went into effect. Muslim and Christian refugee families, fleeing violence and persecution in these now-banned countries, were stranded in airports and customs offices around the world, with little hope for continuing to the United States. World Relief, one of the country's largest resettlement agencies, reported hundreds of refugee families in limbo who needed advocates to rally for reunification with their relatives already in the US. It was painful to see the lack of energy and advocacy for these desperate families. It was the start of a bleak four years for refugee resettlement in the US.

Only the president holds the authority to set national refugee intake numbers, and during these years the annual ceiling hit historic lows. Advocates scrambled to enlist evangelical support in voicing concern for the world's most vulnerable, many of whom were Christians. And while the US previously boasted resettlement numbers of 65,000 to 100,000 per year, our welcome grinded to nearly nothing (50,000 in 2017, 22,000 in 2018, 30,000 in 2019, and 11,000 in 2020).[28] While the United Nations estimated that over 100 million forcibly displaced people were migrating across the globe, our intake numbers told the world, "You are not welcome here. We won't help you. Stay where you are."

But 2021 brought about a surprising and unexpected happenstance.

In the fall of 2021, the Biden administration made the decision to end a decade-long war in Afghanistan by withdrawing American troops from the country. Americans were glued to their televisions as they watched the horrific chaos unfold. With the United States no longer keeping watch, countless Afghans faced death or torture at the hands of the Taliban for their role in helping the US in the Middle East. Thousands of desperate people tried to leave the country immediately; it was unthinkable to be left behind.

So a historic and extraordinary effort was made to evacuate more than seventy-five thousand Afghans from the country.[29] For a brief moment, Americans seemed united in this effort to save people, to get them quickly out of harm's way. Conservatives and progressives alike supported welcoming tens of thousands of Muslim families to the States. While we disagreed about the timing and the execution of the withdrawal, everyone voiced their support for the massive humanitarian lift afoot. Together we *demanded* it.

After President Biden announced America's withdrawal from Afghanistan, the country seemed to experience an interesting turnaround from where it had been just a few years earlier. How could this be, after years of blocking families from predominately Muslim countries? On both sides of the political aisle, the support for these individuals was immediate and surprisingly unwavering.

What changed?

Two things: relationship and rhetoric.

Let me explain.

In 2017 people coming to America from Muslim-majority cultures were framed as *possible terrorists*. Voices on the news insisted they needed more thorough vetting. We were told these families were different from us and would bring an extreme Islamic perspective and religion to the US, inevitably changing American culture. Were these folks *really* refugees—or were they trying to infiltrate the US? We assumed we didn't know enough about them to be sure, so keeping them distant was "appropriate and well-founded."

In 2021 we were told Muslims coming from Afghanistan were *allies*. We had mutual fears and hatred for the Taliban's extremism, as we had experienced their terror in our country too. We knew these families, or at least our military friends and family members did. People we loved fought alongside them and vouched for them, some attributing their very survival during their tours to these individuals. This was personal. We *had* to bring them here.

Both groups of people (those in 2017 and 2021) would be vetted within the same US counterterrorism departments—FBI, CIA, Homeland Security—before arrival and integration into US communities. Both groups were coming from predominately Muslim countries. The difference? The way we talked about them. The way our lives were proximate to theirs.

Instead of seeing Syrian refugees as allies, fleeing their country because of persecution and terrorism, we saw them as a danger, a threat to keep at bay. A different narrative surrounded families fleeing Afghanistan. Our personal experiences and relationships with them made us feel their fears for ourselves and see them like family. Our relationship created new rhetoric.

Desperation from the Northern Triangle

In late 2018, data from US Customs and Border Protection showed an increasing number of women, children, and family units making their way to the border wall. In the 1980s and 1990s, the US Border Patrol was busy curbing the illegal immigration of single adult men, primarily Mexicans in their twenties and thirties looking for economic opportunities. But when America's demand for illegal drugs spiked by 13 percent in 2019, the expanding cartels needed to ensure drug routes. This became an inescapable nightmare for communities and neighborhoods in the Northern Triangle (Guatemala, Honduras, and El Salvador).[30] Hopeful to connect with family already safe and established in the US, large groups of Central American families made their way to the US to seek asylum from the violence they couldn't withstand at home. In December 2018, family member apprehension numbers, 95 percent of which were coming from the Northern Triangle, started to exceed single adult apprehensions.[31]

Migrant caravans through Mexico weren't new, but the numbers became increasingly noticeable and hard to manage along the border. The media started covering the migrations north.

And while not everyone approaching the fence would qualify for asylum, you might be surprised to learn that the majority of families were looking not to *evade* the Border Patrol but to *find* them. They wanted to locate the officers and legally begin the asylum application process. Pictures documented crowds of people standing in line behind Border Patrol trucks, waiting to be vetted by the most powerful nation in the world. They didn't want to cross into the shadows to continue living in fear. They had just traveled thousands of miles to leave the life of hiding behind.

But this is not the story we heard or the pictures we saw. Our headlines and politicians gave us a different framing on their plight. America was swirling with headlines of invasions and migrants coming to take advantage of taxpayer's hard-earned money and benefits. The rhetoric we heard went something like this: *These families are poor and looking for a handout. Who knows how many of them might be violent gang members smuggling kids or drugs or weapons across the border?*

The official response aligned with this negative rhetoric. Instead of creating a functioning system to efficiently vet and process these hopeful and desperate people, we created policies that sought to deter people from being legally processed along the border (policies such as Migrant Protection Protocols (MPP), often called the "Remain in Mexico" program; metering lines at legal ports of entry; and zero-tolerance policy), which forced migrants to wait with their children in dangerous border towns, with no connections or resources and little financial means. We know now that this became a human trafficking heyday for the area cartels.[32]

Desperation from South and Central America

A similar narrative permeated the news when South Americans and Haitians started to arrive at the US border by the thousands. After two devastating hurricanes, many Haitians initially went to South America to find work. After COVID devastated the economy, though, they migrated back north in hopes of working elsewhere. Then, in July 2021, Haitian president Jovenel Moïse was assassinated, and the country fell into economic despair and civil unrest. Where could they go to survive? North.

Conservative headlines in 2021[33] described the Haitian immigrants as poor, dangerous, and uneducated, looking for a handout just as Central Americans always do.[34] So when caravans started showing up in a remote location along the border of Texas, agents corralled them under a bridge in a chain-link-fenced area and quietly deported the majority of them back to Haiti.

Hopefuls from Ukraine

In 2022 another catastrophic and historic event happened across the ocean that stunned the world into welcome. Americans were glued to their televisions, watching in horror as Russia invaded Ukraine. A slow trickle of citizens left the country, then a flood. Millions of Ukrainians became refugees within a matter of hours. Fleeing the violence of the Russian military, cars were packed bumper to bumper on highways leaving the country. In a matter of days, Ukrainians needed new homes, jobs, and communities that would connect them to resources and churches.

The world felt weary but up to the task. Surrounding countries scrambled to welcome millions of desperate families, while thousands of families with financial means boarded flights to other countries, including Mexico, where they could try to enter the US at California's southern border. After years of closed borders (due to COVID restrictions) and insufficient processing resources and personnel, in an expedited and ad hoc fashion, the United States government scrambled to put together a system that processed over twenty thousand Ukrainians at the southern border in a matter of weeks.[35] Within five months of Russia's invasion, the US had welcomed more than one hundred thousand Ukrainians to safety by way of direct flights from Europe.[36] Reporters and news outlets flooded the California borderlands, visiting Ukrainians in Mexico to hear their stories.

Who's Your Neighbor?

Both groups (Central Americans and Ukrainians) applied at the same or similar points of entry, to the same government, for the same or similar protected status. Yet the tens of thousands of Ukrainians were expedited into the US with remarkable speed, while Central Americans were viewed with suspicion.[37]

I wonder what it felt like for those who had journeyed

thousands of miles from Central America or Haiti to see how quickly Ukrainian refugees gained a voice and a place with the American people. What must it have felt like to see others (with noticeably different skin color) processed so quickly? It must have been extremely painful to sit next to someone in a shelter who would undoubtably get into the US before you, even though you had been waiting months (or years) for your own application to be processed. Don't get me wrong, I'm so glad Ukrainians were able to enter easily. I just wish others had a similar opportunity.

You might be thinking, "But Ukrainians were fleeing an invasion. We had a common enemy (like we did in Afghanistan) in Russia."

While this is true, it's hard to ignore the other realities at play. Ukrainians at the border were people with financial means; they were European and white. Central Americans were and are *also* fleeing common and violent enemies: gangs, drug wars, corrupt governments. Americans don't like these enemies either.

Violence is violence. Fleeing a credible fear of persecution based on their race, religion, social status, class, or political affiliation qualifies someone to apply for refuge in the United States under international and federal law. Yet thousands are turned away under broken border policies and made to wait months, sometimes years, on the Mexican side of the border in dangerous cartel territories.

How do we get to the point where we see people's fleeing of violence differently? How do we justify our welcome of Ukrainians and explain away our dissent toward Central Americans, Haitians, or South Americans?

Does it at least make you a bit curious?

But these people (Ukrainians and Afghans) are our friends; they're like family.

And *this* is how we get there.

How we think and talk about people—and how we allow our friends and family to talk about people—changes the way we see people. These narratives, the labels and the rhetoric given to us by the media or well-meaning friends, limit our compassion toward others. They create a justification for our disinterest in certain people's circumstances.

Before we know it, we hold resentment and annoyance for people we've never met.

Without even realizing it, we have a long list of "non-neighbors."

Christlike Welcome

We've already examined our Bibles, revisiting what God thinks and feels regarding immigrants and refugees. We've read how God wants us to act in response to any person in need. Let's open our Bibles again to see what narrative it gives us about our neighbor.

God calls each of us beloved: "I have loved you with an everlasting love; I have drawn you with unfailing kindness" (Jer. 31:3 NIV).

He labels us "children of God": "See what great love the Father has lavished on us, that we should be called children of God! And that is what we are!" (1 John 3:1 NIV).

The narrative we've been given as Christians is that each and every human being is "wonderfully made" (Ps. 139:14)!

Is this how we think about our "non-neighbors"?

Do we value their dignity and the sanctity of their lives?

Do we see them as beloved by God, and therefore beloved by us?

Do we speak about them as children of God, and therefore our brothers and sisters—even though they are strangers?

Do we believe they are wonderfully made, with incredible potential and plans bestowed on their lives just as our own?

These are questions we must grapple with as we examine the narratives that shape our views on immigration. The narratives some of us have been fed about immigrants and refugees don't reflect the narrative the Bible gives us about the dignity of all people. This isn't an easy or comfortable conclusion to reach. After all, if our partisan politics are flawed and we can't readily trust the narratives we've been given, where do we turn? How do we get this right?

As Christians, we have one narrative to prioritize, one that should eclipse all the others vying for our attention. We have a perfect example of how to welcome, because we follow Christ. Jesus came to clear a wider path than his own people were able or willing to walk. The path had grown too rigid, too restrictive, and frankly too corrupt. The religious leaders of the day had become a brood of vipers, tying up cumbersome loads on the shoulders of many while never lifting a finger to help (Matt. 12, 23). Jesus insisted that they were shutting the door to the kingdom of heaven in people's faces (Matt. 23). He called the religious leaders blind hypocrites. But in Matthew 5:17–48 Jesus tried to recalibrate the hearts of his followers with a series of "You've heard it said" instructions. He implored people to turn the other cheek, go the extra mile, give beyond reason, pray for and love those who persecute you, get rid of anger and judgment. He sat with thieves and spoke with sinners.

He humbled the wise, touched those with diseases, ripped the curtain, and overcame death. Jesus was moved to compassion because he loved people. Jesus did all this to demonstrate a different kind of welcome. He asks this of us because he did all of this for us.

Sadly, our culture consumes and continues to spread a different narrative. This narrative—that it is okay to look at someone else as less worthy of being our neighbor, as less deserving of the good things we have—is one Christians should have rejected centuries ago. God's people have always seemed to struggle with this concept. Who is worthy of our time? Who should be included? Who is really worthy of welcome? The answer is at the heart of our own individual redemption with God.

The question is no longer, Who should we welcome? but instead, What is *Christlike* welcome?

Lisa's story

In November 2021, a friend who works in resettlement social work reached out to tell me that the very first family from the Afghanistan evacuation would be arriving in our city after staying for several weeks at a nearby military base. They'd be here in a few days, and she asked if I'd be willing to help welcome them.

To be fully transparent, she said, "I don't know what it will look like. I can't tell you what to expect, but I know it will be inconvenient and financially burdensome." My husband and I decided to take the leap anyway. Being one of the first faces they saw upon arriving in our community would be an honor.

We had recently renovated a studio apartment at our home for visiting guests, and it became the temporary home of this new family (Saad and Taara), who, to our surprise, were expecting a new baby within a few months.

Our friends joined us in welcoming the couple, surrounding them with a support team. Our friend Lee Ann took Taara to all her prenatal appointments and agreed to be her labor and delivery support person. It was a tough and long labor, but Lee Ann was there for every moment. She was there as our new friends welcomed a beautiful little girl into the world.

Saad and Taara are now a family of four and live in a 650-square-foot one-bedroom apartment as they rebuild their lives in the United States. I miss having them in our home, where we could share meals and visit more frequently, but I'm so glad they are getting settled in our community.

The gospel response to the refugee crisis is to welcome them and come alongside where we can. We meet needs just as Christ meets needs. But it's not easy. The nitty-gritty is messy; it's inconvenient. And yet it is our calling. I have found so much blessing in that. I have new friends I never would have had before. We were simply asked to meet a need, and I can't imagine my life without them. Our community is receiving more immigrants and refugees, and I simply think of them as our wonderful neighbors.

The question isn't whether they should be here. The question is what kind of neighbor you want to be. One that represents Christ? Christ followers cannot and should not turn a blind eye to those he has put in our midst.[38]

Discussion Questions

1. Before reading this chapter, what did you know about immigration law in the United States? What did you learn? Did anything surprise you?
2. What do you remember about Syrians and Afghans coming to the United States? What about Central Americans and Ukrainians?

3. What was your perception of who comes to the US border and why? Has that perception changed after reading this chapter? If not, what factors have formed your perceptions most?
4. Which areas covered in this chapter would you like to learn more about?

what does christlike welcome look like?

Unless you live near the US-Mexico border, the closest you (and most Americans) get to migration dynamics is probably through the news and social media stories. In the past few decades, the US has felt constant pressure to curb the immigration of people coming to America through its southern border. People fleeing corruption, violence, and economic instability journey to a country they know offers stability, opportunity, and hope for a new life. It was in a shelter near the Texas border where I met Alicia (name changed), a young mother who had started her journey to the US out of a desperate need to find health solutions for her son with cerebral palsy. She knew he was dying, but no one could help her in her home country. She left her two younger children with her sister and decided to travel to the border wall and plead mercy for temporary passage for medical treatment. Even if she would be denied entry, she knew she had to try. She'd never forgive herself if she didn't.

Drawing by a shelter guest of a mother and her son with cerebral
palsy who presented at the US-Mexico border asking for medical help.
Unable to get the help he needed, he died in her arms in Mexico.

Unfortunately, approaching the border with this kind of
desperation alone doesn't allow entry. It's not the way our system works. As she described her experience of pleading with
Border Patrol agents, she pulled out pictures to show me and
started sobbing. "I showed them my son. They turned me away.
My son died in my arms three days later." The truth is, when
you're standing along our southern border, you can literally see
hope in the nearby landscape. Through the fence line, across
the horizon, you can see it, and it feels so very close. Hope is
what Alicia clung to. It's this hope of a new life that compels so
people many to come.

View from the kitchen window of a shelter in Ciudad Juárez, Mexico. You can see the United States from here. The mountains are stateside. So close and yet so far.[1]

But responding to the humanitarian crisis at our southern border is no easy task. Migration is a global dynamic, and internal displacement (within home countries) and international displacement (outside of home countries) is a worldwide challenge. As of 2022, over 103 million people worldwide are currently displaced and have been forced to flee their homes.[1] Among them are nearly 32.5 million refugees (people forced to leave home because of persecution, war, or natural disaster), around half of whom are under the age of eighteen. There are also millions of stateless people, who have been denied a nationality and lack access to basic rights such as education, healthcare, employment, and freedom of movement.[2]

How would Christ respond to this crisis? How should a Christ follower respond? Unfortunately, we can't simply let everyone who approaches the border enter the US. Our country isn't equipped to accommodate the large numbers of people who wish to live here, and not everyone coming to the border has good intentions. Vetting is needed and extremely important. This is not an open-borders conversation. Choosing Christlike welcome, particularly along the border, is complex, but it's worth examining. Is it possible to have safe and secure borders (for the flourishing of people on both sides of the fence) and compassionate care of people who present themselves to our agents at the border? I believe so. This isn't an either/or conversation, but rather a both/and. Loving our neighbors well forces us to carry this tension.

While discussion about immigration easily veers toward partisan legislation and political solutions, we want our hard-line perspectives to be in better alignment with Christ, not a politically partisan platform. In this chapter, we'll keep the steering wheel steady in one particular lane. As Christians, we must continue to view immigration as a biblical issue, not primarily a political one. Our lane alert must be on to keep us from veering off course, and our navigation should be programed to get us closer to Christ. It will be challenging, and we'll likely need to readjust the wheel a few times so we don't cross lanes.

There is much to consider, but first we must wrestle with this reality:

How we choose to see people directly affects our willingness to attach worthiness to their existence.

This willingness to attach worthiness is directly linked to our desire to welcome others as Jesus did.

How Would Jesus Welcome?

One foundational thing that separates Christianity from other belief systems—our God from other religious figures or frameworks—is Christ's welcome. In Jesus we find a welcome that no one is worthy of and yet everyone is offered. This is a radical concept that no one fully comprehends. None of us qualify for Christ's welcome, and nothing we'll ever do can earn it. Jesus holds out an invitation so radical that his closest friends and the wisest Jewish leaders struggled to grasp it.

The disciples thought Christ came to make them more powerful, to solidify their "chosen" status in the world—that the welcome he offered would elevate, establish, and preserve their own greatness but be tempered toward "others." The disciples were caught several times arguing about who Jesus would name the greatest or who would be allowed to sit next to him when he sat on his throne (Luke 22:24–27; Mark 10:35–45).

But instead, Christ's welcome made his disciples servants to literally everyone they encountered. "Whoever would be great among you must be your servant, and whoever would be first among you must be your slave, even as the Son of Man came not to be served but to serve, and to give his life as a ransom for many," he told the woman and his disciples (Matt. 20:26–28).

This kind of welcome made the Pharisees and religious leaders uncomfortable, frustrated, and angry (Matt. 9:11; Mark 2:13–17; Luke 6:11). But Jesus didn't come to build or preserve an empire. He didn't have time for such things. "Render to Caesar the things that are Caesar's," he said (Matt. 22:21). He was busy expanding a different kind of kingdom: "I must be about My Father's business" (Luke 2:49).

And what was an essential part of that work? Welcoming others.

This is how he spent his time on earth. Jesus's ministry was radically geared toward welcome.

Who Is Welcome?

As Jesus traveled from Galilee toward Jerusalem, "tax collectors and sinners were all drawing near to hear him. And the Pharisees and the scribes grumbled, saying, 'This man receives sinners and eats with them'" (Luke 15:1–2). So Jesus started teaching in parables. Luke records the stories of the lost sheep, the lost coin, and then the parable of the prodigal son. Let's take a closer look at that last one. You can find it in Luke 15:11–32.

The parable features three main characters: a man and his two sons. The opening verses tell us that the youngest son, apparently having grown restless, asks his father for his share of his future inheritance. Then, when he'd gotten his portion, the younger son "gathered all he had and took a journey into a far country, and there he squandered his property in reckless living" (v. 13). When his funds run out and famine sweeps over the land, he becomes desperate. One day, he finds himself envying the pigs he's been hired to feed, since they have enough to eat and he doesn't, and he realizes he's hit rock bottom. Suddenly, living at home with his dad and brother doesn't sound too mundane after all. "How many of my father's hired servants have more than enough bread, but I perish here with hunger!" (v. 17) he thinks. Then he makes a decision: "I will arise and go to my father, and I will say to him, 'Father, I have sinned against heaven and before you. I am no longer worthy to be called your son. Treat me as one of your hired servants.' And he arose and came to his father" (vv. 18–20).

When you read this story, do you ever sit with the idea that it was the son's desperation that drove him back to the father, not his willful desire? What a humbling experience to eat with the worldliest of people and then with pigs. To pick yourself up and drag your wayward feelings and your weary feet back to your homeland. "But while he was still a long way off, his father saw him and felt compassion, and ran and embraced him and kissed him. . . . 'Bring quickly the best robe, and put it on him, and put a ring on his hand, and shoes on his feet. And bring the fattened calf and kill it, and let us eat and celebrate. For this my son was dead, and is alive again; he was lost, and is found'" (vv. 20, 22–24).

Whatever the son was expecting upon his arrival couldn't have been this response, especially since he had rehearsed how to ask his father to become a servant in the fields instead of reinstated into the family. But even from afar, the father recognized this family member, his son. All the correction and criticism he was entitled to give was never given breath. Instead, he affirmed the life and heritage of his son, even to others' dismay.

Now his older son was in the field, and as he came and drew near to the house, he heard music and dancing. And he called one of the servants and asked what these things meant. And he said to him, "Your brother has come, and your father has killed the fattened calf, because he has received him back safe and sound." But he was angry and refused to go in. His father came out and entreated him, but he answered his father, "Look, these many years I have served you, and I never disobeyed your command, yet you never gave me a young goat, that I might celebrate with my friends. But when this son of yours came, who has devoured your property with prostitutes, you killed the fattened calf for him!" And he said to him, "Son, you are always with me, and all that is mine is yours. It was fitting to celebrate and be glad, for this your brother was dead, and is alive; he was lost, and is found." (Luke 15:25–32)

Is it not convicting that many of us more readily identify with the older brother? We're more like the one who believed the father was being taken advantage of. The one who kept his own nose to the grindstone and remained steadfast. The one who was loyal to his father. Many of us who've done it the "right way," followed all the rules, or were born into privilege are upset. Not only are we upset, but we also refuse to join in the celebration that God himself is hosting, to share in the joy of welcoming someone into a new and better way of life. In the case of immigration, we often let our entitlement stand in the way of celebrating our brothers and sisters—our neighbors—who have left home out of desperation, experienced intense hardship, survived horrific journeys to make it to the US and now are getting a miraculous chance at a different life.

But if we side with the older brother for too long, we'll never see the younger son from the father's perspective. Remember what the father says to his son: "It was fitting to celebrate and be glad, for this your brother was dead, and is alive; he was lost, and is found" (Luke 15:32). God is ready and eager to welcome those who are "undeserving." I realize the prodigal teaching is about a son who intentionally squanders everything and is welcomed back from a life of sin. Revisiting this story is in no way meant to imply that immigrants live more sinful lives than any of us in the US. I challenge you for a moment to view it from a different angle: as a story of a person in desperate need of being seen, looked for and sought after, and welcomed with compassion and care to a place of privilege and good standing.

Remember what Paul told the early Christians? "For by grace you have been saved through faith. And this is not your own doing; it is the gift of God, not a result of works, so that no one may boast." (Eph. 2:8–9). Instead of wondering if someone is deserving of your grace, your mercy, your fattened calf, remember that *you were undeserving*. But even so, God constantly looked forward to the day he would welcome you. Aware of who you were and the desperation that was surely part of your life, he turned his eyes and ears to the direction you would undoubtedly come from and eagerly awaited your arrival. He kept his eyes on the horizon. When he saw you from afar, he ran to you. He wasn't afraid to get close to you. He embraced you. He gave you a ring and the best robe, symbolizing your membership in the family. He gave you sandals to alleviate the pain in your body and visibly elevate your social status. And while you were still fumbling through your explanation, the reason for your arrival, he was already hollering at the community to prepare a feast to revive you, to welcome you.

My point is this: The grace we've been given by Christ should be the grace we give others. Everyone makes the grace list. Everyone is to be shown mercy.

Yes, everyone.

The woman caught in adultery, the man swindling and exploiting his community, the person persecuting Christians, the thief on death row—they all were granted mercy.

Paul wrote to the Christians in Rome about this need to extend mercy, saying:

> We who are strong have an obligation to bear with the failings of the weak, and not to please ourselves. Let each of us please his neighbor for his good, to build him up. For Christ did not please himself, but as it is written, "The reproaches of those who reproached you fell on me." . . . May the God of endurance and encouragement grant you to live in such harmony with one another, in accord with Christ Jesus, that together you may with one voice glorify the God and Father of our Lord Jesus Christ. Therefore welcome one another as Christ has welcomed you, for the glory of God. (Rom. 15:1–3, 5–7)

Luke tells us that "the Pharisees, *who were lovers of money*, heard [Jesus's parables], and they ridiculed him. And he said to them, 'You are those who justify yourselves before men, but God knows your hearts. For what is exalted among men is an abomination in the sight of God'" (Luke 16:14–15, emphasis mine).

Jesus called out the Pharisees for their love of money. Why did he do this? Maybe because he knew that the root of their ridicule wasn't that *he* was out of line but that *they* were. The Pharisees had priorities. Power, prosperity, and prestige were at the top of their list. He knew this and rebuked them for it.

Much of our American culture is wrapped up in these things too. We must stay sober-minded about how easily they can also become our own personal priorities.

A Costly Welcome

Jesus's welcome must have been confusing for people in his day. His willingness to interact with those everyone else rejected— the "tax collectors and sinners"—was unheard of in a culture with such an established social hierarchy and ridged customs; it simply wasn't something people did. Christ's welcome was truly radical.

Christlike welcome is no less radical today. To follow him by loving our neighbors requires a constant resetting of long-established comforts and structures in our lives. To reset to his will, some things will need to break. This realization, this process, can be painful. What Jesus asks us to do is hard. There's a cross to carry if we follow Christ in this way. Take a minute to think about who is currently on your "non-neighbor" list. Who is outside your welcome? What kind of unexpected compassion— particularly to immigrants—would raise your friends' or family's eyebrows? What is on your "I could never do that" list? Whom does that exclude, exactly? It's worth pausing for a moment to consider these questions.

Contrary to much of popular American evangelical culture, being a Christian is not supposed to be about living comfortable, curated, and cushy lives. If anyone tells you otherwise, they have an agenda, and it's most likely a selfish one. Following the way of Jesus promises us peace, not comfort; joy, not satisfaction; hope, not earthly guarantees.

Our lives are not to be about us. At some point we should feel the intense neck pain of navel-gazing at our own lives for too long. We were not made to live this way.

We were made to be *wrung out* for each other—giving, loving, and welcoming in such a way that the world takes notice and is therefore drawn to Christ.

Christians should be the ones wading through the gutters of life to find those whom the priests, the city council members, and the elected officials have all overlooked. We ought to live in a way that makes everyone around us ask, "Wait, why are you doing this? Why do you care?"

When's the last time you heard anyone in secular culture or media talk of how impressed, blown away, or wonderfully surprised they were at the church's response to the *fill-in-the-blank* issue? We Christians attend church and confess our sins continually because we know we are an imperfect people. Our communion tables remind us that our sin keeps us outside Christ's welcome but that his bodily sacrifice brings us back into right standing.

So here's my question: *If Christ's welcome toward us cost him his life, and we are to be like him, why would we think our welcome toward others wouldn't cost us the same?*

It's sobering to think that our predisposition to preserve our comfort, to remain complacent and unbothered by our neighbors' burdens, is the sin that prevents us from welcoming those Jesus loves. It prevents us from being like Christ.

Much of our approach has become too calculated, not wanting to lose congregants.

. . . too defensive, not wanting to be "owned" by media narratives.

. . . too fearful, not wanting to be taken advantage of.

. . . too snarky, not wanting to come across as ignorant in the face of opposition.

Church, we are called to more.

We *are* more.

We are *made* for hard things.

We *belong* in these messy margins of life.

How do I know? Because Jesus did these things, and he told us to go and do likewise. He welcomed people from sketchy and unsafe places where neat and tidy answers didn't apply, and seeing people, loving them well, was the priority. The parable of the prodigal isn't the only example of his welcome. Throughout the New Testament, Christ welcomed people by the way he approached their individual situations.

Christ welcomed those society and culture deemed unworthy:

- The Samaritan woman (John 4:1–45)
- The adulterous woman (John 8:1–11)
- The thief on the cross (Luke 23:39–43)
- Tax collectors and sinners (Matt. 9:9–13)

Christ welcomed those with broken lives:

- The prodigal son (Luke 15:11–32)
- Saul, the great persecutor (Acts 9:1–19)
- His friends, including the one who would betray him (Matt. 26:17–25)

Christ welcomed those with physical needs:

- Those who are poor or in need (Matt. 5–7)
- The paralytic (Matt. 9:1–8)
- The woman with a disabling spirit (Luke 13:10–17)
- The man with a withered hand (Luke 6:6–11)

Christ's welcome offered mercy before shame:

- Zacchaeus (Luke 19:1–10)
- The sinful woman (Luke 7:36–50)

These examples only scratch the surface. We could read story after story of Christ's merciful welcome.

Upon Jesus's death, the "keep out" curtain was torn in the Most Holy Place (the innermost part of the temple, where ancient Jews believed God's presence was encountered, but only by the high priest one day a year). It was a dramatic symbol that the previous ways of approaching and pleasing God had changed. God was making a way for those who had been long overlooked and yet always deeply, deeply valued. This new way of welcome *literally* shook the foundations of the earth. Don't miss the importance of this, because as his followers we now must tear down our curtains too. We have to be approachable and available. To love God (according to Matthew 25) we should be radically serious about loving our neighbors.

It was in Jesus's death that we received welcome.

Have you ever thought about what Jesus went through to welcome us into his kingdom? He had already made a place for us in the garden of Eden, one that we mismanaged and were exiled from.

And yet he died to make us a new people, to give us a new culture and a new home.

He did it for you. For me. For "them."

For each of us.

That's important to remember: Christ went out of his way to welcome us. When we were far away, when we were still in sin, doing it all the wrong way, he invited us in (Rom. 5:8).

God got close.

Jesus left his place of privilege to come near us, to wade into all the messy tension he knew we'd drag with us to our seat at the table. And for this the world's most powerful and influential people would mock him. He would be accused of blasphemy, of getting too close to the wrong issues, the wrong people. He would find himself lonely and isolated. But this was all at the request of his Father. God's will was that everyone make the grace list.

Yes, even *him*. Yes, even *her*.

Jesus made his entire life about welcome. If we claim to follow him, we should be busy doing the same.

Are We Extending Welcome?

As the director of a Christian immigrant advocacy community, I can tell you many amazing stories of welcome toward immigrants and refugees in the US. It's one of the things that keeps me going. I wish we all could hear only those stories and never the hard ones. But the truth is, there are many places where we're getting this welcome work wrong. And we can't love people better until we know about the hard stuff—the things we don't want to believe we're capable of, as shown in the following story from a couple of children who arrived from El Salvador and got caught in a system, here in the US, that I never believed possible.

EXHIBIT 41

I came from El Salvador with my brothers who are 11 and 19 years old. I am 15 years old. We came to be with our mother, who lives in the United States, because the gangs were threatening us. They came to our house and beat up our aunt, so we had to leave before they came back.

They took our older brother to another facility and then brought my younger brother and me here to the Clint Border Patrol Station two days ago. At first, my brother and I were together, but then they said that he could not be in the same room.

Michelle's story

A Border Patrol agent came in our room with a two-year-old boy and asked us, "Who wants to take care of this little boy?" Another girl said she would take care of him, but she lost interest after a few hours, and so I started taking care of him yesterday. His bracelet says he is two years old.

I feed the 2-year-old boy, change his diaper, and play with him. He is sick. He has a cough and a runny nose and scabs on his lips. He was coughing last night, so I asked to take him to see the doctor, and they told me that the doctor would come to our room, but the doctor never came.

The little boy that I am taking care of never speaks. He likes for me to hold him as much as possible.

We live in Room 203 with 25 children. I estimate that it is about 10 feet by 15 feet. The first night, I slept on the concrete ground and used the blanket to cover me because it was so cold. I could not sleep because I was so cold and my head hurt. Yesterday, some of the girls left, and so I was able to get one of the beds. Last night, the little boy and I were able to sleep in the bed together. Today a nurse got mad at us because a comb is missing. Two girls asked to use a comb, but only one was returned. We are not allowed to keep combs, so they came in and took out all of the beds and all of the blankets in order to punish us. Now we will have to sleep on the floor.

In our room there are two toilets and a sink. One toilet is out in the open, and the other is in a stall with no door, so there is no privacy when we go to the bathroom. There is no soap.

We eat in the same room. Some of the children have to eat on the floor. I have to change the little boy's diaper on the bed.

Since arriving here, I have never been outside and have never taken a shower.

I, M. Z. L., swear under penalty of perjury that the above declaration is true and complete to the best of my abilities. This declaration was provided in Spanish, a language in which I am fluent, and was read back to me in Spanish. June 18, 2019[3]

This is one out of many stories made public and entered as Exhibit 41 (a legal term for evidence) in a legal proceeding to evaluate whether the US government was and is providing adequate living conditions for children in our care. What led to the US government needing to care for children in the first place? Let me offer you some background information.

First, I'll clarify how the asylum-seeking process works.

US and international law state that you must be *within the country from whom you're requesting asylum* before you can apply for asylum in that country. You *cannot* apply at a consulate in your home country or at a US Embassy. You aren't expected to be carrying any particular form or papers. If you're coming by land, there are two main ways to seek asylum: present yourself at a legal port of entry *or* "illegally cross" an international border and *then* ask to apply for asylum. Asylum seekers cross our borders to find our officers and begin the legal, internationally agreed upon screening and application process. Stepping onto US soil between ports of entry is *a legal way to seek asylum in the US*.

In the summer of 2017, the US instituted policies that made life much more difficult for asylum seekers. At the direction of the Trump administration, the Department of Homeland Security piloted a new zero-tolerance policy within the El Paso, Texas, Border Patrol sector. White House memos and congressional reports[4] changed the border enforcement practices and implemented a zero-tolerance policy requiring the Department of Justice to prosecute all adult immigrants apprehended crossing the border illegally. Previously this wasn't the usual practice.[5] Illegal crossings were now to be consistently punished in federal criminal court as a misdemeanor charge, instead of just dealt with in civil immigration court. Those illegally crossing the border between ports of entry to seek asylum with their children were no longer distinguished from those illegally crossing the border seeking to evade authorities. No exceptions were to be made for those looking for Border Patrol to start a legal process for protection.

Zero tolerance was one of many ways the Trump administration tried to curb migration at the time, by separating parents from their children to "deter migration" to the US and lessen the burden of processing asylum claims.[6]

Piloting the program was a quiet operation at first, but in April 2018 the policy began full implementation along the southern border sectors, increasing family separations without any functioning mechanisms in place to reunify parents and children. Many parents were criminally charged and then deported back to their home countries without their children, leaving thousands of kids in US detention centers and shelters or foster homes and extended family placements within the US.

> During the six weeks the policy was active, DHS separated 2,816 children. . . . In 2019, DOJ disclosed the separations of an additional 1,556 children prior to the zero tolerance policy but also during the Trump Administration. . . . In the period since the zero tolerance policy was effectively paused in June 2018, at least 1,000 additional children were separated, bringing the total reported number of separated children to between 5,300 and 5,500.[7]

It was a mess—an inhumane deterrent experiment that turned into a full-blown, traumatic humanitarian crisis. News outlets filmed and photographed thousands of babies, toddlers, and children screaming and crying as they were taken out of the arms of mothers and fathers who had carried them thousands of miles to escape the hardships and trauma in their communities back home. This is how the most powerful nation in the world—a country many see as a Christian nation—"welcomed" these weary and vulnerable families legally seeking help in the United States.

Every immigration processing system was overwhelmed by this change of enforcement. Cement holding cells built in the 1980s and 90s to house single adult males illegally crossing were packed with women and children.[8]

BUT OBAMA BUILT THE CAGES!

Some of the most common pushbacks I hear about this horrific situation shift the blame to previous administrations. "Obama built the cages!" "This rule was already in place. Trump just enforced it."

The simple answer is this: not all laws are just or humane, as this season showed us. Just because someone built the cages does not justify our continued use of them. Christians shouldn't be okay with the use of cages, within any administration. It's disturbing that we would try to defend the use of them at any time in our nation's history. We should have held President Obama's administration to a higher standard, the same as President Trump's.

The more complex answer is this: crossing the border without permission between ports of entry is, technically, against US law—in most cases, a misdemeanor offense—but federal law enforcement authorities historically have used discretion in when to criminally charge an individual with unlawful entry. This sort of discretion is common in law enforcement: a police officer has the legal authority to ticket every driver who exceeds the speed limit, but in reality they consider a number of factors: How fast was the driver going, one mile per hour over or fifty over? Was this the driver's first offense, such that a warning might be appropriate? Does the officer have time to issue a ticket, or are they too busy chasing down a more serious, violent criminal offender? And was there a compelling reason that the driver was speeding, such as transporting a child experiencing a medical crisis to the emergency room?

Similarly, federal law enforcement officers generally

use discretion in when to charge an individual with the misdemeanor offense of unlawful entry. Under most administrations—Republican or Democratic—they generally would *not* criminally charge an individual who crossed the border without inspection but who was actively *looking* for (not running away from) Border Patrol to seek asylum, which US law explicitly says is one lawful way to begin an asylum case (even if the crossing itself was unlawful). They generally also would not criminally charge adults when they were accompanied by small children, precisely because that would require the child to be separated from the parent. They would instead detain and process them under civil immigration laws, either deporting the whole family together or allowing them to begin an asylum claim, without filing criminal charges.

But the Trump administration's declaration of "zero tolerance" for unlawful entry meant that, even in these very sympathetic cases, parents were charged criminally and their children were taken from them.[9] Human beings made in the image of God were held in cages, sometimes packed next to one another like animals. Surely we can't continue to justify why we allowed this to happen when news outlets made it clear that cages were still indeed being used.[10]

One of the facets of US immigration policy is a set of national guidelines and standards that ensure the humane detention and dignified treatment of immigrant children while in the care of federal agencies. These strict regulations are called the *Flores* Settlement Agreement (FSA). In June 2019, during a routine evaluation trip to the facilities holding children, monitors tasked with determining whether detention centers were in compliance with FSA, as well as a team of lawyers, interviewed children detained at two adult jail facilities in Texas (Clint and Ursula). A medical professional conducted physical and mental health exams of some of the youngest children being held.[11] Many of these lawyers had visited immigration detention centers dozens of times before. This wasn't their first experience. But it *was* the first time they saw conditions so egregious that they decided to break their confidentiality agreement and take these stories— testimonies from children—to the press.

After hundreds of interviews, it was clear that violations were occurring in every category of FSA protections, including the length of stay in detention facilities, unhealthy and over- crowded holding areas, lack of access to healthcare, clothing, hygiene products, food and nutrition, and temperature control.[12] Customs and Border Patrol officers randomly selected children and brought them to a conference room to meet with these lawyers. (The lawyers did not choose which children they would meet.) The testimony you read previously was just one of these stories.

The separation of families and the detention of children continued until Christians, along with other Americans, raised their voices demanding the zero-tolerance policy end. Under intense political pressure, President Trump ordered the prac- tice to cease in June 2018, though some separation of families continued to occur.

I remember the first time I talked with a father and the daughter he had been separated from. We met at a shelter in Juárez, Mexico. I was walking around the courtyard of a Catholic shelter and began chatting with a group of ladies who were smiling over hot coffee they had made in the community kitchen. As I asked about their journeys to the US, their stories quickly turned to their experiences in US detention. All of them spoke of the cold cement floors and freezing air. "Two meals," they told me. "But rice wasn't cooked, and hot dogs were frozen. That's what they gave us."

I asked if anyone had been separated from their children, and several older women turned to the youngest in the group. Standing in flip-flops, she signaled with a small wave of her hand, "Me."

"Ve a buscar a tu papá" (Go get your dad), they told her. In a minute, she returned with him and stood in front of me. Gustavo, my translator asked, "You were separated?"

To which the dad nodded. "I didn't know where they took her or when I'd see her again. But what could I do? We couldn't go back."

Standing with a group of women and a father who was separated from his teenage daughter when crossing the border to seek asylum during "zero tolerance."

I asked his daughter how old she was and what it was like. She told me she was thirteen and it was frightening. She didn't understand why she couldn't stay with her dad. She was put with other children and had to help take care of the small ones, all of whom were strangers to her.

I asked if they knew in advance that they would be separated. They both shook their heads.

"Where are you from, and why did you decide to come?" I asked. They were from Honduras, and the rest of their family still lived there. They hadn't seen them in months. This young girl was his eldest child, and she had just turned thirteen. She was incredibly beautiful, and the gangs in their area back in Honduras had noticed her. Once she turned thirteen, gang leaders informed her father that she was to be a girlfriend for them. The father couldn't let this happen to his daughter. He refused; they threatened his life. So this man and his daughter left their family (their wife/mother and two younger sons/brothers) behind to seek safety in the United States. They didn't want any part of gang violence, yet, "If we would have stayed, she would have had to do this. I couldn't let that happen. But we get to America, and they take her from me. Why? She's just a child. I was scared. She was scared. I didn't know the US was like that. These were the hardest days of my life."

I know what you might be thinking. They needed to separate them to make sure he was indeed her dad, that she wasn't being trafficked. I'm with you. That step is important.

But this isn't the way to do it, to detain them separately for weeks with no communication, explanation, or understanding of what was taking place, cramming them in cells and cages, feeding them frozen food, giving them no indication as to when or even if they'd be reunited.

Put yourself in their shoes and imagine, for just a minute, what that would be like. Imagine fleeing to protect your daughter from such terrifying harm, and the most powerful nation on earth—whose leaders campaign on their faith and family values—treats you in this way.

We can do better. We *must* do better. As Christians, we should be actively advocating for different solutions—humane ones—and holding our elected officials to a higher standard.

Extravagant Welcome

Did you know that the word *prodigal* (according to the Oxford Dictionary) has more than one definition?

1. Spending money or resources freely and recklessly; wastefully extravagant.
2. Having or giving something on a lavish scale.

Reading through these two definitions makes me wonder about Christ's intended purpose in his parable of the prodigal son. Was he telling a story about a prodigal son or a prodigal father?[13]

While we tend to assume the first meaning defines the son and the second his father, I'd like to suggest that both definitions could very well represent the father. Depending on your Bible's translation, the title above Luke 15:11 might read *The Parable of the Prodigal Son, The Lost Son,* or *The Compassionate Father.* Isn't it interesting to think about this story from a different angle—the one of the reckless Father?

The father—who represents God's searching, open-armed welcome in the story—welcomes his wayward son so extravagantly, so freely, that it angers his most loyal son. One son was careless yet repentant, the other reliable yet angry. The father approached both of them, offering the same invitation to each.

Through his death, the Son of God extends this same kind of reckless welcome to us. He made a path forward for those who can't make a way for themselves—*and that's all of us.*

People who have no means, no good works, no social status or citizenship; those who had no justification to approach the throne of God now have access. Isaiah 64:6 says we have *nothing, not even our good works,* to offer God. We're all going to show up at his throne and simply plead the blood of Christ, and God will separate us *by the ways in which we saw and took care of our neighbors* (Matt. 25:31–46).

To the tax collectors and sinners, this kind of welcome was lavish. To the Pharisees, it was wasteful. But this is the welcome Christ came to give: a radical, lavish, seemingly wasteful yet always free invitation to all.

If Jesus welcomes us with joy and peace in the midst of our sin, meeting our physical and spiritual needs when others naturally criticize, showing us mercy and alleviating our fears before he demands anything from us, how does that reshape the way followers of Jesus should welcome others? Does his death define our welcome? It should. His welcome wasn't a cheap offering, and it certainly didn't come without pain. It made a powerful, life-changing way forward that changed the entire world.

This is life-changing welcome.

Sherene's story

On a cold, snowy night in November 2004, I went to my first Thanksgiving dinner. It was in Rochester, Michigan, and we were going to the home of my husband's uncle and aunt. We bundled ourselves and our little twenty-two-month-old son and drove thirty minutes from our tiny one-bedroom apartment to the first American house we had ever been inside. We had been in the United States for only about two months, and everything still felt strange and unfamiliar.

I experienced my first Thanksgiving meal, the kind I had only seen pictures of in magazines before. There were mashed potatoes, cranberry sauce, stuffing (I still have no idea why it is called stuffing; I've only seen it in a casserole), gravy (very confusing to an Indian), bread rolls, sweet potatoes, and green bean casserole. But of course, the roasted turkey occupied the place of honor at the head of the table. On the sideboard were apple pies, pumpkin pies, and pecan pies. I had never eaten pie before, and I am biased, but Michigan has amazing apple pies!

In addition to all these delicious Thanksgiving favorites, there was still more food on an extra table. There was mutton biryani, chicken curry, yogurt raita (salad), a basket of chapattis (Indian flatbread), and chicken pepper fry. Our family being Indian, we couldn't leave the Indian delicacies from the Thanksgiving meal. They are an integral part of our culture. While we embraced the American traditions of the Thanksgiving feast, we also did not want to forget our country of origin and the food we ate during celebrations there. So if Thanksgiving was to be a day of remembrance and gratitude, we needed to introduce the flavors and spices of India to the meal.

Since that day, I have celebrated many Thanksgiving meals. I learned to prepare all the dishes over time, except for turkey. As immigrants, we easily assimilated and accepted the culture and traditions of the country we moved to, but we couldn't leave behind or forget the traditions we had grown up with—they are a part of our DNA. Throughout our lives, we are all constantly being formed. As an immigrant, I had to find the balance between living by the country, culture, and people who had formed me for the first twenty-six years of my life and adapting to the new country, culture, and community that was forming me.

What about you? Look at your circle of friends, family, and community; whom can you invite to sit at your table? Perhaps they could bring a meal with a blend of spices that marries well with turkey and gravy. Let us be willing to open our hearts and our homes to those who do not look like us, who might not share much in common with us, but who still want to be seen, known, and loved. After all, people are people.[14]

Discussion Questions

1. How would you define Christlike welcome?
2. What role does a Christlike welcome play in immigration policy? What about in our own neighborhoods and communities?
3. Is there a story in the Bible of God's lavish love that stands out to you?
4. What specific steps could you take to welcome immigrants, refugees, and other at-risk neighbors in your community?

CHAPTER 6

why do people come?

In his home country of Honduras,[1] Miguel and his brother owned a neighborhood barber shop and lived with their families in a small apartment. The apartment walls were thin. Day after day, week after week, the mother of the family next door would leave for work. And every day, Miguel and his brother could hear awful things through the walls. They knew the young girl in the apartment next door was being abused by her father.

One morning, the brothers heard things they couldn't ignore. They rushed out of their apartment, kicked down the neighboring apartment's door, and raced inside. One of them held the father down, away from the daughter he'd been sexually abusing, and the other ran for the police. When the police arrived, they called the mother and took the father into custody.

The brothers were relieved. They were glad the girl was safe. They knew it was the right thing to do.

But a few days later, the brothers started receiving death threats. Unbeknownst to them, the neighbor they had tackled was a local gang member. Barging into his home, calling the police, and having him arrested was unacceptable. Miguel and his brother were now on "the list." Over the next several weeks they received frightening calls at their barber shop and experienced drive-by shootings. One day, while Miguel was out buying a drink at a shop around the corner, gang members drove by the barber shop and shot his brother in the neck. Miguel returned to find his brother bleeding out on floor.

His brother was rushed to a nearby hospital and remained in a coma for weeks. With the shop in shambles and medical bills piling up, Miguel faced the burden of supporting his own young family (wife, daughter, and a baby on the way) *and* his brother's family, particularly as they all had targets on their backs. No place was safe. Security guards were positioned outside his brother's hospital room.

Miguel took a job with a local politician, helping to organize campaigns. But the threats resurfaced, this time attached to pictures showing where his wife was and where their daughter went to school. Miguel constantly feared for his life and his family's lives. The danger was so intense that the politician he worked for advised him to flee. "Maybe that will take the heat off your family," the politician said. So with this advice, Miguel fled to the US in hopes of applying for asylum; once this was secured, he would send for his family.

Historically, asylum seekers could walk across the international bridge between Mexico and the United States and turn themselves in for vetting and a "credible fear" test with asylum officers.[2] But by this time, the Trump administration had implemented metering policies along the entire border,[3] requiring people to wait in cartel-run border towns on the Mexican side of the border until their name and number were (hopefully) called. The borders were teeming with people like Miguel— people who had fled danger, violence, and persecution. Yet they weren't allowed to plead their cases for safety in the US, as the law allows.

Listening to Miguel share his story about his life and the lives of his family being threatened by gang members because he and his brother saved a young neighbor girl from abuse.

Miguel graciously related his story to me and the group of American women I was with during our visit to a shelter in Ciudad Juárez. At that time, Miguel had been waiting just over three months. His money had run out. He had nowhere to wait safely. Without the help of the church shelter that took him in, he would likely be dead.

He teared up as he spoke of how hard the entire situation had been on his marriage. "It's hard to explain to my wife why I risked everything to save a stranger," he said after explaining that his wife had given birth to their child while he was here waiting for entry. "She's mad at me for doing this, for being stuck here, but I thought leaving would be safer for them. I can't do anything but wait."

"I'm a Christian," he told us. "I believe God wanted me to save that girl. But doing so has made things so hard. I'm not with my wife and kids. I've never held my new baby daughter.

I've lost my brother. Why? We saved that girl from that man, but it cost me everything."

At the Paso del Norte International Bridge in Ciudad Juárez, Mexico, this cross stands as a symbol against the region's gender-based violence against women. The sign reads: "Ni Una Más" ("Not One More").

The narrative we're often told in the US is that the people waiting at the border are people we don't want in our communities. We're told that the men coming to our border are rapists and criminals. Yet wouldn't you feel better knowing men like Miguel were in your neighborhood?

Later that day, the walk back to the United States—across the international bridge between Ciudad Juárez, Mexico, and El Paso, Texas—felt uncomfortably long and depressing. I noticed a long line of men standing along a chain-link fence under the bridge near the processing station. They were standing directly in the hot sun, their faces weary and tired. Miguel was in a line just like this one a few months ago, hoping to be seen, heard, and given a chance at a new life. Instead, he was expelled into Mexico without anyone hearing his story. The images we see on the news never tell the whole story that each person carries within them. Miguel changed what I see in these images. He gave me a spiritual gut check that increased my compassion and curiosity.

Each of the men standing beneath me as I walked over the bridge had a story—maybe not one like Miguel's, but a story that brought them to a desperate line of hungry, tired people, hoping the most powerful nation in the world would show them mercy. Not all of them will be able to stay. Not all of them *should* stay—I know that. But here is something else I know: each of them is a valuable creation of God, and God cares about their stories. God welcomes them with a standard that transcends the laws of borders and nations. Furthermore, many of them are our brothers and sisters in Christ, and we must consider this.

Many of us feel angry or frustrated that thousands of people approach and cross our borders each month. I wonder, where has our curiosity has gone?

Asking Why

Aid organizations are sometimes criticized for addressing only symptoms of a problem instead of the source of the problem. As the story goes, there comes a point where we need to stop just pulling people out of the river. We need to go upstream and find out why they're falling in. The conversation about the US's southern border often falls into a shouting match between two sides: those who want to stop asylum seekers from getting in and those who want to make a way for them. And while each position makes strong points and passionately believes in its own virtues, both are essentially presenting different answers to the question, What should we do about all the people in the river?

The time has come for Americans to ask a new question. Instead of asking what we should do, we should ask, Why are so many people coming to our border? What factors are leading to this humanitarian crisis? What would I be hoping for as I approached the doorstep of a powerful nation like the US?

We don't have to guess. International humanitarian organizations have been researching this question for decades and have identified a number of common "push" and "pull" factors, as explained by The National Immigration Forum:

> Individuals around the globe migrate for a broad variety of reasons, which can be conceptualized in two general terms: "push" and "pull" factors. "Push" factors are conditions in migrants' home countries that make it difficult or even impossible to live there, while "pull" factors are circumstances in the destination country that make it a more attractive place to live than their home countries. Common "push" factors include violence, gender inequality, political corruption, environmental degradation and climate change, as well as lack of access to adequate health care and education. Common "pull" factors include more economic and work opportunities, the possibility of being reunited with family members, and a better quality of life, including access to adequate education and health care.
>
> Although the general "push" and "pull" factors describe motivational trends and patterns, they do not account for the specific and personal reasons for migrating that are unique to every individual.[4]

Every time I visit the borderlands, talk with my Uber driver (who is usually an immigrant), or read a testimony of someone in immigration court, I find that everyone has a unique story. No two are the same, but they fall into certain categories that can help us understand why so many people continue to come.

Things That Push

Helping people in their home countries

A few years back, for a video resource Women of Welcome was creating, I interviewed Jo Ann Van Engen, the cofounder of an incredible ministry in Honduras called Association for a More Just Society. I asked Jo Ann how we could help people in their home countries. "How do we help them stay?" I asked.

"Nobody takes on this journey without thought," she said. "It's a really difficult decision."

Have we considered how difficult the decision must be? What does it take for someone to leave their family, home, language, and history to travel (sometimes) thousands of miles to a new country? Our news-cycle narratives present an over-simplified story, one that doesn't take into account the costly and complicated reality of showing up at America's doorstep.

Reality hits hard when you realize there's no welcome mat waiting for you along the southern border.

As Americans, we have a hard time imagining making a decision this difficult. We live in a country of options. For many of us (particularly those with economic privilege), if we don't like our neighborhood, the education our children receive, the local tax rates, or the state government that shapes our communities, we have choices. We can move to a different neighborhood, a new city, or even a different state. We simply migrate within the US to find a way of life we believe is worth living. We often switch schools or campaign and vote for new leadership without fear of violence or death. We are a mobile society. Living in the same town you grew up in is becoming less common. Opportunities for change are abundant, and we're always on the move to chase our dreams.

But leaving *everything* we've ever known is not a typical American story. It's hard to imagine the kind of pain entailed in the decision to leave one's homeland behind entirely. Jo Ann continued, "No one wants to leave their home country. Leave their families and houses, their memories and language. When they do leave, it's because things are so bad they feel they don't have a choice."

What are those things?

There are a few common points of desperation people are trying to escape.

Desperate Poverty and Lack of Opportunity

What would you do if you couldn't find a way to feed your family? First Timothy 5:8 says that a person who doesn't provide for their own household is worse than an unbeliever. But we don't need the Bible to tell us that; the drive to ensure that our children and families survive is one of the most powerful and universal experiences in life. Many, many migrants are on the move because they are searching for a way—*any* way—to provide the basics for their families.

Many Americans have layers of resources standing between them and true destitution. Even if you were to become unemployed for years, you would probably have community, church, or family relationships to help make ends meet. Failing that, you would have government and nonprofit programs to help fill in some gaps. Those who face total destitution, however, have usually long since depleted these safety nets—or never had them to begin with.

Many people live off the land, relying on their hard labor to provide food from the ground. If crops fail due to famine, natural disaster, or industrial pollution, many have no cushion to fall back on, and entire communities can be destabilized in a matter of weeks. Others who work in towns and cities face poor wages and lack of job opportunities. Some fear they can't provide for their children in the short term; others look ahead and realize that without education, their children and grandchildren will face the same vulnerabilities. "It's a series of vulnerabilities that make people desperate to migrate to the US for better opportunities," Jo Anne explains.

Chronic Violence, Persecution, and Lack of Safety

As we saw in Miguel's story, in many countries systems of oppression and violence surround regular citizens, and the danger can be impossible to avoid. Innocent and vulnerable people are caught in the middle. Drug trafficking is one significant cause in which the US is not innocent. In the 1980s, cocaine use skyrocketed. Most of the world's cocaine is produced in South America—Bolivia, Peru, and Colombia—and most of the market demand is in the United States. What countries are in the middle? The Northern Triangle countries and Mexico are caught up in the middle of the violence the drug traffickers create in bringing their product to market. Traffickers work to establish and maintain trade routes and to keep rival competitors at bay. They kill people who get in their way or won't cooperate.

Another major contributor to violence is gangs, who maintain a strong presence and control poor neighbors, extracting "war tax" from the residents (meaning part of your earnings go to placating the gang leaders). Everyone pays rent. Innocent and vulnerable men, women, and children are not complicit, but they are continually caught in the middle. Who wouldn't try to go live somewhere safer? These same areas tend to be full of corruption and lack accountability; authorities can be bought. Elected officials have stopped doing their jobs for the community or the country. Their greed and power-hungry tactics further contribute to poverty and violence and push people out. And you can add national disasters and political and national unrest to the list of "push" factors encouraging people to leave their homes searching for a new life in the US.

Love

Ultimately, it's *love* that motivates many migrants to leave their home and the country of their ancestors to seek a safer life for themselves and their family.[5] Jo Ann helped me understand this. It's one of the first things she told me when I asked to understand these dynamics better. People love their families enough to risk seeking a new life and a brighter future.

If they make it to the US, immigrants often send money back home to support family who couldn't make it out. This provision may pull them out of poverty or enable them to find housing in a safer neighborhood where children can go to school rather than be coerced into joining gangs or selling drugs—or worse. Far from wanting to come and destabilize the United States, many of these mothers and fathers have taken such risks and costs to find safe, stable neighborhoods and communities where they can contribute and thrive.

Things That Pull

Despite our wildly disparate policy history (as we saw in chapter 4), a Pew Research poll reported in August 2020 that the United States has more immigrants than any other country in the world.[6] Now that we've considered the factors "pushing" people away from their home countries, let's talk about what "pulls" people to the United States. In many ways, the US seems to offer the solutions to many desperately felt needs.

Economic Opportunity, Safety, and Stability

We advertise ourselves as the country of freedom and opportunity, welcoming and open to all. Compared with the communities immigrants are leaving, the US often has more employment opportunities, higher wages, stabler and safer communities, and more resources and services for raising a family. I've heard dozens of parents' stories at migrant shelters, and there are several constant and strong themes. Two stand out: safety for their children and the ability to work to feed their families.[7]

Family and Community

For some, family or community members are already established in the US, so there is hope of making a smooth transition into belonging, and access to a better quality of life.[8] Leaving everything behind is easier if someone you know is willing to help you get assimilated, connect you with a church, or help you find an honest job. All of this feels attainable if others have found success and have settled into a new and better livelihood. If you spend any time at all with immigrants, conversations quickly turn to talk about family, where other members are, and how long it's been since they've seen them. When I've talked with a group of women who clean homes in my neighborhood, all of them mentioned family "back home" that they haven't visited in years. "It's taken fifteen years to get a green card for my mother, and we're still waiting. I need to stay here and work, and I am nervous that even with my green card I couldn't get back. I don't trust the system. The rules are always changing. It's very confusing, but I hope I see her before she dies."

A Destination Worth the Risk

While violence or poverty may push people out of their homes, and the hope of freedom, safety, and opportunity pull them specifically to the United States or Canada, the journey itself is full of additional dangers and trouble. When you consider the dangers people are willing to face to undertake this journey, you begin to understand the power of the push and pull factors they're experiencing.

Each year, an estimated half a million Central American migrants jump on freight trains exporting goods and products north, trains that enter the United States from one of several locations. This journey is dangerous for many reasons. The people must ride above the packed freight cars, risking dismemberment or death if they fall (or are pushed off by the crowds, cartel members, or thieves) during the long, multi-country ride. But also, gangs and organized-crime syndicates often control these export routes and extort passengers along them. Kidnapping, sexual violence, and forced recruitment are common along these lines.[9]

Others, especially Caribbean migrants such as Haitians, follow a different route to the United States. Pushed out by all the same factors—including natural disasters such as hurricanes and the 2010 earthquakes, and lack of resources for survival—many have already made the flight to countries in South America such as Brazil, Argentina, or Chile. Most Caribbean men and women who attempt to migrate to the United States first spend an average of ten years working and building a life in their new South American country. Then, as the need arises, they walk north, often passing through multiple countries on the way to our border, including Ecuador, Peru, Colombia, Panama, Costa Rica, Nicaragua, Honduras, Guatemala, and finally Mexico. This journey is incredibly dangerous. In addition to the health and safety concerns inherent in walking the length of an entire continent without shelter, food, water, or healthcare, many are robbed, assaulted, and raped. Women often miscarry pregnancies along the way.[10] The hope of honest work, safety, and an opportunity for a fresh start, one without fear around every corner of your community—this is what makes the risk worth it.

"Just Get in Line"

As we get to know people like Miguel, whose story was at the opening of this chapter, and we recognize the terrible push and pull factors that result in their journey to our border, our compassion grows. When I ask myself, "What if my child's life or health were in danger? or "What if I couldn't feed my family with the work or sustenance available in my country?" I realize I would do *anything* for them—even undertake a risky and perilous journey.

This realization is why many like Miguel can't or don't apply for a visa, waiting their turn and coming safely and legally.

Why don't people just get in line?

Let's take a moment to talk about what it looks like to "get in line." What avenues are available for people looking to legally enter the United States?

Contrary to popular assumption, the US-Mexico border doesn't account for even half of immigrants arriving in the United States. India, China, Vietnam, and the Philippines also top the list.[11] Whether someone is from Africa, Asia, Europe, or the Middle East, they have to take a journey to eventually arrive in the United States—a physical journey, but also a journey of paperwork and patience. Many arrive first at a refugee camp as they seek asylum or paperwork to immigrate to the US. For those coming from across the pond, bureaucratic approval is as essential as a boat.

US immigration policies are generally based on family-linked or employment-based reasoning and values. At the moment (and until immigration reform is passed by Congress), people immigrate to the US through one of these four avenues:[12]

- blood (family)
- sweat (work)

- tears (asylum/protection from persecution)
- luck (lottery)

Blood is the avenue that asks, Do you have family in the US? *Sweat* asks, Are you able to work when you get here? Since the Immigration and Nationality Act of 1965 was passed, the two key factors opening the door for someone to come to the United States are having family members who are US citizens or lawful permanent residents or an employer willing to sponsor the immigrant. These two values—family and work—create the foundational values of immigration policy.

But not all family and not all jobs are eligible. Only a spouse, parent, child, or sibling can sponsor a person's immigration application, not aunts, uncles, grandparents, grandchildren, or cousins. The jobs eligible for visa sponsorship are specialty occupations requiring significant education and proven success in niche areas of technology, engineering, university professorships, law, and healthcare. The person has to meet these specific job placement needs; there are no "sweat" visas available.

Tears asks the question, Are you persecuted? In 1980 another small category opened up to would-be immigrants called the US Refugee Admission Program, which allows the United States to protect and welcome those who are fleeing persecution and have nowhere else to go. But persecution is narrowly defined for those seeking refugee or asylee status. They must prove they can't return home specifically because of their race, religion, nationality, political opinion, or social group membership. Those fleeing poverty or violence that is not motivated by these categories do not qualify.

As you can imagine, most people who want to come to the United States do not have qualifying family members to sponsor them or a specialty degree that awarded them a job with an employer willing to apply for them. Most do not suffer the specific types of persecution that qualify someone as a refugee, and only a tiny percentage of those who do are accepted specifically by the United States. This is where *luck*—via the diversity lottery system—comes into play. The State Department makes an additional fifty thousand visas available each year. But these aren't for just anybody, and they aren't first come, first served. To apply, a person must meet certain criteria, including citizenship in a country the United States deems underrepresented in our current diversity mix. But most of the countries of origin of those we encounter at the border (Mexico, El Salvador, Honduras, Haiti, Venezuela) don't fit this criterion. Even if the person meets the criteria, in recent years, the odds of winning a visa in the diversity lottery have been between one in two hundred and one in five hundred, depending on the number of entries.[13] So for every one person who comes to the United States this way, 340 who are eligible to apply have tried and failed.

Now that we understand these four avenues—blood, sweat, tears, and luck—let's think about which avenue might work for someone like Miguel.

Miguel does not have a mother, father, sibling, or spouse in the US to sponsor him. That eliminates one avenue, blood. Even if he did have family in the US, his situation is dire, and family-based immigration takes years. Miguel doesn't have years; he's living day-to-day, trying to stay alive, stay safe, and reunify with his family, who is struggling without him.

While Miguel intends to work hard and earn money if he makes it through, he does not have the unique skills, training, or contacts to be sponsored by an employer. Many industries in the United States rely heavily on immigrant workers, including agriculture, healthcare, manufacturing, food service, and more. Yet these kinds of jobs are rarely eligible for a work sponsorship; there are very few legal ways for companies to hire the immigrant workers they need. That eliminates the second avenue, sweat.

Although Miguel is fleeing violence, he is not a refugee so long as he remains in his country of origin, which is the first way to come to the US on account of "tears." And even if he were to flee to a neighboring country, very few individuals from Honduras have been selected for resettlement to the US. He earned a target on his back because he protected a child from a gang member, not based on his race, religion, or nationality. He *might* argue that he fits into a "particular social group," but if he wants his case considered, he will likely need to make it to the US border to seek asylum, which is the other way that one could qualify for permanent legal status on account of "tears." Finally, coming from Honduras, he is not from an underrepresented country and can't apply for the diversity lottery. Even if he were eligible, his odds of getting in would be only 1 in 340 (the precise odds vary year to year based on how many applications are received). So that eliminates the fourth and final avenue, luck.

Miguel couldn't stay where he was, as the gangs controlling his community intended to destroy his livelihood and take his life. His wife, daughter, and new baby have no safety or future there either. He is being pushed out of his home. The safety, work opportunity, and freedom found in most communities in America pull him to our borders, but he can't apply to come through the blood, sweat, tears, or luck avenues. So he took the only path he thought he could: crossing the border to apply for asylum.

But upon making his application, which is a legal thing for him to do, he was sent to Mexico—which is not his country of citizenship—to fend for himself and hope his case is eventually called so he can share his story and request asylum in the US.

The odds are stacked against someone like Miguel. In recent years, about three times more Hondurans were denied asylum in immigration court than were granted it.[14] "Just getting in line" suddenly isn't so simple.

When Home Is the Mouth of a Shark

Christians must be a people moved to compassion, as Jesus was, willing to look past media stereotypes to learn real stories of real people, to understand the push and pull factors that have created this crisis, and to work together to find effective, safe, and humane solutions.

After visiting a shelter for Somali refugees in London, Warsan Shire (a British-Somali poet) was inspired to write the poem "Home" after hearing the stories and horrific realities of these beautiful refugees far from home. It starts like this:

> no one leaves home unless
> home is the mouth of a shark

I recommend you listen to the poem in its entirety, here:

I'm convinced that our compassion for a person is tied to our curiosity about them. When we see caravans of people approaching our borders, or long lines of individuals waiting to be processed by our border officials, I pray we first see them as image-bearers, as

"Home" by
Warsan Shire

human beings, as brothers and sisters. Because we believe they are made in God's image, I hope we hold our frustrations and judgment at arm's length and remain curious. People all around the world have been on the move since the beginning of creation. People will always be migrating for one reason or another. I pray we would ask good questions—questions that help us think about ways we can show up well and be a blessing. Often when we hear these people's circumstances, we want to help, we want to know what the solution is. We'll discuss that further in chapter 9. Until then, let's keep leaning in. Let's keep welcome front of mind.

Alex's story

Alex was born in one of the most dangerous states in El Salvador. When he was just nine months old, his parents fled the country and moved to the US because of death threats and poverty, making them unable to provide for the family. Alex was raised by his grandmother and his uncle.

He grew up hearing story after story of gang violence and extortion: gangs would threaten business owners and other people, telling them to pay money if they wanted to live. Some of Alex's friends knew of a gang that murdered a person just for having a nice pair of shoes. His friends by the river would often find bodies floating in it. Reporting violence to the police in El Salvador was useless, as gangs essentially governed much of the country.

Alex's parents tried to move back to El Salvador a few years after losing a house in the US. They sent money to his uncle to buy them a house, but on the day he was going to buy it, gang members kidnapped him. His uncle survived, but the gang took the money for the house and started sending regular threats; this time the target was Alex.

His parents got a call. The person on the other end of the line demanded weekly payments for Alex's safety. They knew everything about Alex: where he went to school, what time he left and entered the school, and even the bus he took. Alex knew he had to leave El Salvador.

But his life-threatening troubles weren't over yet. Just thirteen years old, he nearly lost his life multiple times on the way to the United States. The first time, he nearly drowned on his way from El Salvador to Guatemala. He had to go through a river with a strong current, but he didn't know how to swim.

The current dragged him downstream, and he washed up on the shore, unconscious. He knew then that the "seven- to fifteen-day trip" would be much, much longer. It would end up taking three months.

The next time he nearly died, he was in Mexico. Gang members came to where he was staying and held him at gunpoint as they told him to get into their car. He was questioned about his trip. They ended up letting him go instead of taking him with the several other people they had rounded up. This moment, Alex remembers, was a testament to God's protection over his trip.

The rest of the journey was perilous and dangerous, but at every step of the way, God was with Alex. Eventually, after crossing the border, Alex was reunited with his parents, but they were strangers to him. He hadn't seen them since they left him as a baby.

Over the next few years, Alex worked to become a legal resident and finish high school. Because he was undocumented, it was easy to lose hope, but he continued to push himself every day to obtain a better life for his family and legal standing in the US.

Discussion Questions

1. What are some of the hardest, most devastating situations you have faced? In what ways did your family, friends, and faith community support you during this time? In what ways did they fail to do so?
2. What circumstances might cause you to flee your home?

3. Have you heard information or stories like the ones shared in this chapter on the news before?
4. Had you heard about the blood, sweat, tears, and luck avenues to come to the United States? How does this information change the common request that immigrants "just get in line"?

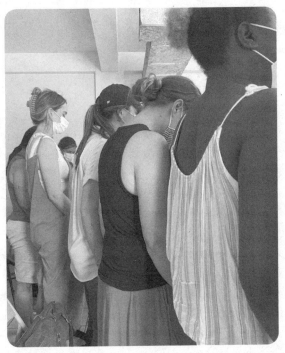

Women of Welcome immersion trip participants visiting and praying with migrant mothers in a shelter in Ciudad Juárez, Mexico.

have you seen this headline?

After I had a couple of immersion trips across the border under my belt, I started talking about my experiences more widely on social media. The responses varied, to say the least. Good friends, even people who had known me since I was a child, started commenting and messaging me with concerns. A former elder of the church I grew up in messaged me in what I could clearly tell (through the frequent use of all caps and stark statements) was anger.

"You keep talking about *these* people as if they're *all* mothers and children," he said, "but they're not. There's more to what's going on at the border. And if *these* people want freedom so badly, they should stay in their *own* countries and fight for it. What about the gangs who come here and all the trafficking of children at the border. Don't you care about *those* things?"

Of course I do. And of course there is more to the story. But what story did he want to hear, exactly? Did I need to explain every broken part of the current system before he would acknowledge any concern for the people suffering at the border?

I messaged him back, acknowledging that not everyone at

the border should be allowed in. I reaffirmed that open borders are not the solution and that thorough vetting is crucial.

Knowing he had a grown daughter with small children, I asked if he might feel differently if her husband was murdered in front of her, leaving her and the kids with little option but to travel north to connect with other family members already in the US—as so many people do. Would he expect her, now a widow and single mother, to stay and take on a corrupt government and a community that couldn't protect her husband? With what resources could she possibly do this? She had lost her provision and protection all in one horrifying day.

No response.

My reply wasn't meant to be a gotcha. I was sincerely asking. I never did hear back. Not later that day, not weeks or months later. Many challenges exist in this conversation. Pain points (perceived or real) like the ones this elder expressed override the compassion I *know* Christians have. Fear changes everything, crippling the mercy Christ commands us to extend. We're to put *people first*. Not just Americans, not just proven allies, and not just people with means. Everyone is a neighbor.

When I look across the landscape of news headlines, I can't help but think of the tens of thousands of well-meaning immigrants—image-bearers created with immeasurable value and potential—who are completely lost within many of the erroneous narratives we find most frightening.

The truth is, immigrants are frightened too.

The vast majority of them never wished to leave their homes and countries, their families and languages, their communities and churches. No one wants to make that kind of journey. No one wants to sell everything they have and pay a coyote to take them thousands of miles through unknown terrain and cities, with no guarantee of safety, survival, or crossing. No family wants to starve for food and thirst for water. No woman wants to endure rape in front of her children.[1] No one wants to find themselves on the doorstep of a foreign country that has pulled the welcome rug from the porch. No one wants to beg for mercy.

While I believe my evangelical community has a deep well of compassion for hurting people, conversations like the one I had with my church elder drain any energy or confidence people have to speak up about such things. Who wants the controversy? Who wants to be trolled or bombarded with all the other narratives, especially if you're not an expert in the issues that swarm this subject? No one wants to take on all those stingers.

After receiving several similar messages from other friends and acquaintances, I realized that cultivating compassion wasn't going to be easy. I couldn't simply share a story or two and find people willing to lament and engage. At first I was distraught, frustrated, even angry with the church—until I remembered there was a time when I too had missed this *by so much*.

My angry commentors are right about one thing: there *is* much more to this issue. Honestly, I don't think I've ever been in an *easy* conversation about immigration, and it's my job to have these conversations. It's a complicated subject, hijacked by partisan politics and agenda-filled narratives. People have gotten lost in the mix. Flesh-and-blood men, women, and children simply become numbers, stats we scan or go-to political wedges.

If it were our own families standing at the fence or waiting in a refugee camp across the sea, we would hope that someone would champion our flourishing. We would hope that Americans would show mercy to our children as well as to our spouses. We would hope they would see us as neighbors. We would hope they would live out their faith instead of falling prey to their fears.

We must listen well. We must remain charitable. When we don't, a conversation can easily turn into a never-ending rabbit trail or a toxic dumpster fire. Neither do what's needed, which is focusing on the image-bearers caught in the middle of these dynamics.

Peering through a section of the southern border wall in New Mexico to see the houses and children on the other side.

When I listen to people talk about immigrants and refugees, the most common thing I hear behind every comment is fear. Fear of a changing American culture, fear of increased violence or economic burdens, fear of terrorism or human trafficking or drugs, fear of America's citizens not getting the help they need, fear of Sharia law taking over cities and eventually the nation. And even though one of the most frequent commands in the Bible is "do not fear," we often fear things we don't understand and people we don't know.

But as Christians, we can't stay there. We all have so much to learn. I'm *still* learning.

To learn, we have to listen. If we listen well, we will have the often dreaded and ultra-intimidating opportunity to address the plethora of peripheral things surrounding the core issue. So let's open the door wide to the most common concerns and pain points nearly every immigration conversation entertains. Let's have the discussion that's necessary to (hopefully) settle our hearts a bit more. This allows us to attach some confidence to our compassion, no matter where we find ourselves in this learning process.

Clickable Headlines

At one time or another we all fall prey to fallacious headlines. Clickbait has a toxic relationship with fearmongering; it's a lucrative and powerful marketing tool, so these days it's difficult to separate fact from fiction. In general, we should never believe we're getting the *full* story from our own echo chambers. Every news outlet has some sort of bias, and it's hardest to recognize in articles shared by your own circle. I read other news outlets not because I agree with them all the time or like their pundits any better than the ones I prefer, but because I'm curious. I read and listen to people who view things differently than I do because I want to understand why we seem to be in a stalemate. Checking in with CNN and MSNBC doesn't lead me down a slippery slope. It's fascinating to try to find the commonalities with other outlets *before* I see the discrepancies. Piecing together a story from various (differing) sources usually gives you a more accurate big picture. Turns out, seeking nuance is not dangerous—it's a prudent discipline. Finding the nuance in each story helps us see people better, and for Christ followers that should always be the goal.

So let's click on some of these headlines together.

Headline: Migrant Caravans Are Invading America

Caravans aren't a new phenomenon. The Bible tells us that our biblical ancestors frequently traveled in caravans when migrating to different lands. Do you remember when Jesus himself traveled in a caravan? It was so large that for three days Mary and Joseph didn't know he was missing! But when news outlets showcase images and continual footage of migrants "pouring across the border," many of us think America is being overrun by dangerous cartels and drug smugglers. We watch stories about huge caravans of people coming up from Central and South America, and more recently the Caribbean. It feels worrisome. *Who are these people? What are they doing? Why are they coming? And is anyone really trying to stop them?* When "thousands are storming the southern border" it can appear that America is being taken advantage of or, worse, being invaded. But caravans don't make for good invasions. If someone was looking to evade the Border Patrol, they wouldn't travel in a large, very noticeable, media-monitored group.

When we use "invasion" language, we're insinuating that every person who presents at the border is coming with violent intent, with guns and other weapons. Think about it: Russia *invaded* Ukraine. Yet our experience with caravans at the border is nothing like the violent threat Ukraine has faced. The truth is that in recent years, the majority of people coming to our southern border (at least from 2019–22 data[2]) have been asylum seekers, who approach the border looking *for* the Border Patrol, not seeking to evade them. But for years we've had a mismatched approach as we continue to meet this *humanitarian crisis* with a *military response*. In 2018, a mother who traveled from Honduras with a caravan approached the border with her toddler-aged children and was tear-gassed. Nearly every news outlet covered the story, as the images were terrifying. *What on earth were we doing?*

She had nothing but diapers and children in her hands.[3]

This type of media coverage also might make you think that under certain administrations we *do* have open borders. The truth is, under no administration (essentially since 1924) has the United States had an open-borders immigration policy, meaning unregulated and unmitigated entry into the country.

One of the first things I expected to hear when I started working in immigration spaces was the push for open borders. I fully anticipated hearing this from every Democrat I encountered. In every meeting, I waited for the "open borders" influence to seep into the conversation under the guise of being the most compassionate approach we should take toward those migrating from neighboring countries. Imagine my surprise when, in hundreds of meetings with advocates, White House officials (in both the Trump and Biden administrations), and hard-line Democrats, the topic was never advocated for. *Not even once.* It's been one of the biggest surprises of my work over the last six years. In fact, I'm not aware of any immigrant advocate—who maintains credibility in this space and is taken seriously—who advocates for open borders. Everyone knows it's unfeasible in terms of American safety or geopolitical dynamics.

While our immigration system (the avenues in which people can legally immigrate to this country) is proving unsustainable and broken from a humanitarian and economic perspective, our country's continued border security has increased. The Border Patrol estimates[4] its effectiveness has gone from apprehending only about one-third of those who sought to enter unlawfully in 2003[5] to more than 80 percent in 2021.[6]

Reports from the last several decades estimate a drastic decrease in "got away" numbers. Illegal crossings do indeed happen, but crossing is vastly more difficult than it was even just a few years ago. This can be attributed to better technology (ground sensors, cameras, drones), more agents (behind cameras, on foot, and in various sky, land, and water vehicles), and increased infrastructure (physical structures, processing facilities, and internal staffing allocations) along the borderlands.[7]

Women of Welcome immersion trip participants
praying over a local border patrol agent.

Yet caravans continue to come. They likely always will. Migrants are extremely vulnerable on these journeys, and for those coming to our southern border, the horrific dangers and violent realities men, women, and children face are well documented. While impossible to know to the fullest and most accurate extent, numerous reports suggest that the majority of women who make this journey are sexually assaulted before they arrive. Without community, connections, much food, or money, someone would rarely make this kind of journey alone.

People travel in larger groups for safety purposes. Bigger numbers mean more protection from outside thieves and abusers.

Often the narrative of caravans being funded by a progressive puppet master pops up. No investigative journalism has turned up any credible stories to support this narrative. In the many trips I've taken to the border, I've heard from a lot of people who borrowed money from family or friends or loan sharks to make the trip, often creating a great pressure to succeed economically upon arrival, to repay their debts. Never once has anyone mentioned that their trip was paid for by anyone.

America is a strong country, and a big country; a couple of hundred people in a caravan aren't going to take over the Border Patrol or the US military. They can and do sometimes overwhelm the system, or a specific border sector, which makes for weary agents, but no one is barreling over the Border Patrol to get into the US.

If you look closely at these images or the footage on your screen, you'll see the thousands of people crossing over and then standing in long lines, waiting to be processed. They aren't looking for trouble—they're fleeing from it.

Headline: Our Vetting Process Is Lacking

Most Americans don't realize the process our country invests in, the lengths we go to, to ensure (as best we can) that those who want to reside in this country are indeed safe and unaffiliated with terrorism. Refugees are the most thoroughly screened people who travel into the United States.[8]

A refugee is someone who has been given the official designation of "refugee" (someone who is confirmed to be fleeing from persecution) by the United Nations and applies for resettlement *from overseas*. Those who are fleeing persecution overseas generally do *not* have the option of choosing where they are resettled. They apply and are given a destination upon vetting approval. They have no idea where they'll be resettled. It could be anywhere in the world. Refugees who are displaced from their homes await their chance for a new life in refugee camps. At any given time, there are over one hundred refugee camps around the world, with the largest ones in Africa and the Middle East.[9] Stats vary depending on the crisis, but the average stay in a refugee camp is ten to fifteen years.[10] If and when a person is selected to be resettled by the United Nations, the vetting process takes an average of two years to complete.

While this book isn't meant to be a thorough read on all immigration policies and vetting procedures, I'll try to explain our vetting process in its simplest form.

This process isn't perfect, but it's pretty darn good. "Numerous checks by several government departments are built into the process to meet all security requirements, resulting in a rigorous, often years-long process, for every refugee who reaches the United States. This vetting ensures that if, at any stage, there is any doubt about the refugee's history, affiliations, identity, or credibility the individual does not enter the United States."[11] "Since the Refugee Act of 1980 established the current refugee resettlement framework, there has not been a single Islamist lethal terrorist attack in the United States perpetrated by an individual who entered the United States through the U.S. refugee resettlement program."[12] That's a pretty good track record.

The 2021 humanitarian lift in Afghanistan was unique and expedited, but the vetting was still incredibly thorough. Families, many of whom the US government had already vetted when they were initially screened during the US military hiring process, waited on military bases for months before getting a green light for temporary humanitarian parole in the US. Vetting processes vary slightly based on how and where one enters the system, but the US conducts meticulous security screenings, which include the following:

- biographic and identity investigations
- FBI biometric checks of fingerprints and photographs
- medical screenings
- other checks by US domestic and international intelligence agencies (Department of Defense, CIA, DHS, FBI)
- refugees from some countries, such as Iraq and Syria, undergo an additional review through the Security Advisory Opinion process[13]

Those who request asylum at our borders have a slightly different vetting process than those who apply for resettlement from overseas. An asylum seeker has the burden of proving that he or she meets the definition of a refugee. "To be granted asylum, an individual is required to provide evidence demonstrating either that they have suffered persecution and/or that they have a 'well-founded fear' of future persecution"[14] in their home country. Persecution is internationally defined as a threat to your life or freedom based on account of your race, religion, nationality, political opinion, or membership of a particular social group. US immigration courts determine whether an applicant meets the requirements of an asylee and is allowed to stay in the US. While poverty is incredibly heartbreaking, it does not qualify someone for asylum. Many asylum seekers will be deported simply because their stories are ones of poverty and not persecution.

It turns out the world has a long waiting list for those needing welcome.

What about False Claims?

Many people assume that the vast majority of those showing up at our southern border are making fraudulent asylum claims.

This type of headline floats around from time to time as migration numbers spike. Here are three things to keep in mind when you see this narrative:

1. Asylum fraud is uncommon:

   There are two different departments responsible for adjudicating asylum cases: U.S. Citizenship and Immigration Services (USCIS) and the Executive Office of Immigration Review (EOIR). Neither USCIS nor EOIR release regular data on the number of cases terminated or investigated due to suspected fraud. . . .

   Claims that asylum fraud is on the rise are unsubstantiated by available data, and often rest on the mistaken assumption that an overall increase in rejections is indicative of a rise in fraud.[15]

2. Not every denied or unsuccessful asylum claim is considered fraud:

   Some applicants might tell a truthful story, but one which simply fails to meet the qualifications for asylum. Or, some applicants' stories might contain minor discrepancies that don't appear to be outright or deliberate lies, but that undercut their overall credibility.[16]

3. The US Government is robustly equipped to assess fraudulent claims:

   Both USCIS and the EOIR have established departments, personnel, and policy dedicated to the detection and prevention of fraud in immigration proceedings. Under USCIS, personnel in the Fraud Detection and National Security Directorate (FDNS) are embedded in asylum offices, working "closely with law enforcement and intelligence community partners" to investigate and resolve potential cases of fraud. FDNS reviews evidence, conducts site visits, produces reports, and can refer cases for criminal investigation. Under EOIR, the Fraud and Abuse Prevention Program (Fraud Program) investigates claims of fraud across the immigration court system and runs a centralized office for receiving complaints related to fraud.

In addition, there are several safeguards built into the asylum process that serve to curb fraud at the outset.[17]

Those Who Cross Illegally

While waiting to apply for and going through the US vetting process can be arduous, it's arguably the better alternative to trying to cross illegally. As mentioned, "got away" numbers have drastically decreased over the past decade because of our increased infrastructure, border enforcement personnel, and technology across the borderlands—but that certainly doesn't mean illegal crossings aren't happening. Those who cross unlawfully are entering without inspection, and Americans are concerned about the risks they pose (terrorism, gang affiliation, etc.). Matthew Soerens and Jenny Yang wrote about this in their book, *Welcoming the Stranger: Justice, Compassion and Truth in the Immigration Debate*:

There has never been a documented case of a terror attack perpetrated by an individual who entered the United States by illegally crossing the US Mexico border. Still, it's certainly not impossible that a would-be terrorist could seek to reach the U.S. by entering the country unlawfully. Particularly in the past few years . . . the likelihood of being caught is high: as of 2017, the US Department of Homeland security estimates that as many as 85% of those who seek to enter illegally are either apprehended or blocked from entering the country.[18]

Another general and legitimate concern is that the millions of immigrants who reside in the US (from crossing unlawfully in past years) have not undergone screening of any kind. Soerens and Yang acknowledge this as well, noting,

> While there is little reason to think this poses a particular threat, especially when most have already been present in the US for more than a decade without doing harm, it is a vulnerability.[19]

It's important to note that about half of undocumented immigrants in this country are from (vetted) visa overstays. Pew Research and NPR have reported on this numerous times, concluding "that persons who overstay their visas add to the US undocumented population at a higher rate than border crossers. This is not a blip, but a trend which has become the norm." . . . "As these numbers indicate, construction of hundreds of more miles of border wall would not address the challenge of irregular migration into our country, far from it." . . . "We have made tremendous progress since the year 2000 in reducing undocumented immigration into this country," the study's author, CMS senior fellow Robert Warren, told NPR.[20]

Headline: Immigrants Are Draining American Resources

Many Americans perceive, much like I used to, that immigrants (particularly undocumented immigrants and asylum seekers) are a massive drain on our economy and take advantage of taxpayer dollars. It's true that there is a cost to local communities, especially concerning emergency healthcare, education, and child food assistance (like SNAP or welfare). But according to economists at the *Wall Street Journal*, it's also true that immigrants use these services at lower rates than native born citizens.[21]

Apart from asylum seekers (who aren't allowed to work in the US for the first six months upon their arrival[22]), Stephen Moore, the economic advisor to the Trump 2016 presidential campaign and a chosen nominee to the Federal Reserve, suggests that regardless of citizenship status, the average immigrant pays "about $80,000 *more* in taxes than they will receive in federal, state, or local benefits over their lifetime."[23]

> While the economic benefits of having immigrant labor are more obvious on the national level, local communities across the country usually spend resources supporting the immigrant workforce. The Federal government has recognized this disparity and has introduced policies to direct national resources to help states with the costs of illegal immigration, but gaps do indeed exist. Nevertheless, immigrants have a generally positive economic effect on public resources and the national economy.[24]

The frustration that immigrants take jobs away from American workers is hard to fully accept, as "help wanted" signs are seen in nearly every store in our communities (at least from 2019–23). We need workers in this country. Yet we complain both that immigrants don't work and are a drain on our services *and* that they work too hard and take jobs from Americans. Both can't be 100 percent true.

Headline: Immigrants Raise the Risk of Crime and Terrorism

While partisan narratives tend to swirl around crime rates and terrorism, innumerable studies have confirmed two simple yet powerful truths about the relationship between immigration and crime: immigrants are less likely to commit serious crimes or be behind bars than the native-born, and high rates of immigration are associated with *lower* rates of violent crime and property crime. This holds true for both legal and unauthorized immigrants, regardless of their country of origin or level of education.[25]

A terrorism and risk analysis done by the Cato Institute over a forty-one-year period found the following:

> Terrorism presents a real threat to the life, liberty, and property of Americans. That has led many Americans to worry about foreign-born terrorists entering the United States, either legally or illegally, and carrying out disastrous attacks. But foreign-born terrorism on U.S. soil is a low-probability event that poses small risks and low costs on Americans as a whole. From 1975 through 2022, the average chance of dying in an attack committed by a foreign-born terrorist on U.S. soil was 1 in 4,338,984 a year, and the chance of being injured was about 1 in 773,938.[26]

President Trump's former chief of staff John Kelly emphasized, "The vast majority of the people that move illegally into the United States are not bad people. They're not criminals. They're not MS-13." Most immigrants come to the US to pursue educational and economic opportunities and have little to gain by committing crimes.[27]

But what about MS-13? Don't they pose a greater threat to Americans if we don't crack down on immigration? Here are a few things to note about the MS-13 gang in relation to immigration. MS-13 was created in Los Angeles in the 1980s and did not originate in Central America.[28] And while some politicians have indicated otherwise, according to WOLA (the Washington

Office on Latin America), "There is no indication that the number of MS-13 members in the United States has increased in the past few years."[29]

MS-13 gang members *have* been found and arrested along the border, attempting to cross illegally into the US in small groups looking to intentionally evade Border Patrol agents. This is why resources along the border are indeed important and necessary. But overall, Central American youth are fleeing gang violence, not bringing it to the border.[30] In most cases, those approaching the border to seek asylum are not hidden gang members posing as family members. Again, from WOLA, "Of all unaccompanied minors apprehended at the southwest border from 2011–17, only 0.02 percent were either suspected or confirmed to have ties to gangs in their home country, according to U.S. Border Patrol."[31]

Immigrant communities are often the targets of gang violence. According to the Law Enforcement Immigration Task Force, "MS-13 relies on networks of its members in Central America to pressure U.S. immigrant communities by carrying out threats against family members back home."[32] The gang primarily preys on a specific community—young, mostly undocumented immigrants—not the rest of the country.[33]

Headline: Immigrants Will Replace American Culture

I have to admit, the idea that immigrants will replace American culture was one I struggled with for a while. It wasn't until I asked my friend Dr. Russell Moore to sit down and help me think it through that I started making progress. Because he is a pastor, theologian, and evangelical leader in this country, I wanted to know if he thought immigrants played a major part in the cultural shifts we were seeing in America. And if so, how should the church respond? Dr. Moore suggested the following:

We need to separate out our response as Christians and as Americans. If we start first as Americans, I find that those who fear immigrants causing some sort of bad change in American life really don't have much confidence in the United States of America and its founding principles. You can go back and look through American history and every single wave of immigrants that have ever come into this country have always experienced this same kind of response, *The Irish are coming in, they don't share our values* . . . *The Italians are coming and are going to bring alien ideas of allegiance to the pope* . . . and so on and so forth. Any wave of immigration has seen these kinds of reactions. But what have we (also) always seen? It's that the people who come to the US are often the people who are most committed to American ideals—it's what brought them here. They are usually the people who are most committed to family structure because they're seeking a better life for their children. . . .

Now, as Christians, the gospel that's been given to us is not to cordon off some cultural norms and to protect those things. It is to go into all of the world and make disciples. And what we have in the US, in many communities, is the world coming to us. We shouldn't be stuck in fear and loathing, but instead be thinking about how we can serve these people, share the gospel with them, and meet their needs. How can we recognize that (for those who are believers) the things they bring strengthen our churches and our connection with the global body of Christ—which is actually to whom we belong.

The apostles wrestled with these same kinds of cultural dynamics with gentile believers in the New Testament. The question essentially was, What do we expect these gentiles to become? Should they be culturally uniform with us? And the answer was no.

Dr. Moore and I chatted for about forty-five minutes about this, and it was one of the most helpful conversations I've had. If you'd like to hear more of our conversation, we recorded it so you can listen in.

Concerns of
American culture
change

Many people are concerned that with an increased population of Muslim immigrants, US cities and the national government may be taken over by Sharia law.

Do we really know what Sharia is, though?

We've seen the extreme use of this Muslim law by terrorists or extremists, so the idea of Sharia law makes us nervous. To be clear, "Sharia acts as a code for living that all Muslims should adhere to, including prayers, fasting and donations to the poor. It aims to help Muslims understand how they should lead every aspect of their lives according to God's wishes."[34]

It's interpreted differently by Islamic leaders, governments, and everyday Muslims. The real question becomes, Do we need to fear its implementation in the United States?

NPR reports that US courts "already recognize and enforce Sharia in everything from commercial contracts to divorce settlements, to wills and estates," much like the courts recognize these aspects for Christians.[35]

The system in the U.S. is similar to Britain: Courts are open to honoring agreements made under Islamic (or Christian, or Jewish) law and worked out by religious tribunals—within reason. As Marc Stern of the American Jewish Committee told NPR, U.S. law supersedes religious agreements when those agreements are seen as grossly unfair. For example, when a Muslim husband in Maryland argued that he should be allowed to give his wife nothing when they divorced, citing Islamic law, the courts ruled that he did not have the right to do so.[36]

It's possible that a greater Muslim presence in the United States would have *some* impact on the law. Christian-backed blue laws, which limit the sale of alcohol on Sundays to foster religious observance, are a good example of such religious influence.

But considering there are perhaps two million Muslims in the United States, a country with a population of more than 330 million, fears of an outbreak of Sharia law seem overblown. Even if there is somehow a serious push for the imposition of Sharia—or any other religious law—it would quickly run up against the first amendment to the Constitution, which ensures that no religious tradition can be established as the basis of laws that apply to everyone, including any form of Sharia, Christian canon law, Jewish halacha, or rules of dharma from Eastern religions.[37]

Headline: Immigration Is a Major Venue for Human Trafficking

People who leave their home, friends, family, and community behind are uniquely susceptible to exploitation by traffickers and smugglers. Undocumented immigrants are especially vulnerable to human trafficking because they are afraid of their traffickers and often threatened with deportation if they speak with US authorities about their circumstances. According to the ACLU, "In the United States, victims of trafficking are almost exclusively immigrants, and mostly immigrant women."[38] "The U.S.

Department of State estimates between 14,500 and 17,500 victims are trafficked within the United States each year."[39]

Often people conflate human trafficking with human smuggling, so it can be helpful to know there is a big difference. In its simplest form:

- Human trafficking is a crime against a person and centers on *exploitation*. Modern day slavery includes forced or coerced sex trafficking and/or labor, debt bondage, or slavery-like practices for commercial or personal gain.
- Human smuggling is a crime against a state or country and centers on *transportation*. It involves the importing of people across national borders, intentionally evading immigration authorities while harboring/transporting noncitizens.

"Not all individuals who are smuggled are trafficked, and movement is not required for trafficking to occur."[40] Those who are smuggled are moved by private vehicles, buses, vans, trucks, and planes. It's become a lucrative business for the cartels; lucrative for the cartels, deadly for migrants. Every migrant experiences some sort of trauma before or after they approach our fence line.

"No one crosses the border for free," one migrant woman told me. "You either pay with money or your body. Most of us have run out of money by the time we get to the border."

According to the Human Trafficking Institute, even though a strong link exists between immigration and human trafficking, the two issues are often compartmentalized to allow bipartisan human trafficking legislation to pass without being burdened by hotly contested immigration policy. However, this practice greatly hinders anti-trafficking efforts by divorcing two interrelated issues: increased border security and ad hoc policies (like Title 42, a public health code during COVID, and MPP, short for the Remain in Mexico Program).[41]

While Border Patrol agents are equipped to evaluate fraudulent family claims and identify victims who are being smuggled, our broken immigration system and shrinking legal pathways ensure that this lucrative and evil exploitation of people not only continues but grows. The harder is it is for people to "make it to freedom," the more desperate people find themselves, choosing between horrific options in which no one wins but the cartels. The truth is, the more legal pathways the US offers, the less business we give to traffickers and smugglers.

Again, I'm not suggesting the US take everyone that wants to come, but surely we can do a better job of providing options that undercut the cartels and give families more options. Christians are strong advocates for those stuck in human trafficking. This is one of our strengths. One of the best things we can do to win the war against modern-day slavery is to use our voices to pass immigration reform, as the two systems are deeply intertwined.

Headline: Immigrants Smuggle Large Amounts of Drugs

A recent (2022) NPR/Ipsos poll showed that many Americans believe migrants are the biggest transporters of illegal drugs into the US.[42] It's true that fentanyl overdose deaths are up in recent years and that much of the US fentanyl supply is smuggled through the border. But experts say most of the fentanyl and other illegal drugs are smuggled through official (legal) ports of entry, hidden in large trucks and passenger vehicles, while a relatively small amount is smuggled by cartels across the border between those ports. Virtually none is smuggled by migrants themselves, says Victor Manjarrez Jr., a former Border Patrol sector chief who's now a professor at the University of Texas at El Paso. "The probability that they're going to carry some kind of illicit narcotic is probably close to zero," Manjarrez said. "The vast majority of that fentanyl is going through a port of entry."[43] This reality suggests it's not that more Border Patrol agents are needed between ports of entry, but that more robust screening technology, customs and border personnel, and accountability measures at legal ports of entry is the better solution.

Should American Needs Come First?

America first! It's a common phrase that's become popular in the past few election cycles, fueling many conservative pundits and podcasters. As an immigrant advocate, I always hear, "With all the needs here in America, shouldn't we prioritize the needs of American citizens first?" While I do believe it's important for any country to take care of its citizens, I think the best way to answer this question is to do so from a *kingdom* mindset, as a scriptural perspective will help us recalibrate our thinking.

Prioritizing needs in the United States

First, we'll need to take off our well-intentioned "empire mindset" and put that aside. We are Christians first and foremost, therefore a "kingdom mindset" is what should primarily shape our hearts and minds. It is our heavenly citizenship (and our allegiance and obedience to God) that should take precedence over any national citizenship we (or our neighbors) have or don't have here on earth. A kingdom mindset will help us think about our neighbors and see them as God sees them.

Too much talk of "empire" (or "America first") will have us justifying things we Christians were never meant to defend.

The world is in too much pain for us to put our compassion on limited supply.

In Matthew 22:36–39 the Pharisees are looking to test Jesus. They ask him, "Teacher, which is the greatest commandment in the Law?" Jesus replies, "'Love the Lord your God with all your heart and with all your soul and with all your mind.' . . . And the second is like it: 'Love your neighbor as yourself'" (NIV).

We are to love God and to love others. And every person you see, American or not, is in that "others" category.

As we've seen, the Old Testament has a plethora of verses that elevate care and concern for orphans, widows, sojourners, and those in poverty. So we know God has special heart and concern for them. But when we look at the whole of Scripture, our framework is the greatest commandment, to love God and to love others. This framework gives us the freedom to enter into any space where we see a need, whether that be in our home country or in a foreign country.

Remember Jesus's teaching on the mountainside as described in Mark 6:34–44 (NIV):

> When Jesus landed and saw a large crowd, he had compassion on them, because they were like sheep without a shepherd. So he began teaching them many things.
>
> By this time it was late in the day, so his disciples came to him. "This is a remote place," they said, "and it's already very late. Send the people away so that they can go to the surrounding countryside and villages and buy themselves something to eat."
>
> But he answered, "You give them something to eat."
>
> They said to him, "That would take more than half a year's wages! Are we to go and spend that much on bread and give it to them to eat?"
>
> "How many loaves do you have?" he asked. "Go and see."

When they found out, they said, "Five—and two fish."

Then Jesus directed them to have all the people sit down in groups on the green grass. So they sat down in groups of hundreds and fifties. Taking the five loaves and the two fish and looking up to heaven, he gave thanks and broke the loaves. Then he gave them to his disciples to distribute to the people. He also divided the two fish among them all. They all ate and were satisfied, and the disciples picked up twelve basketfuls of broken pieces of bread and fish. The number of the men who had eaten was five thousand.

Do we trust God to meet our needs as we follow his command and his example to have compassion on everyone in the crowd before us? Do we believe he will bless us, our families, our communities, and our nation if we follow him in this way? Do we believe he will supply all our needs?

Again, in Matthew 9:36, Jesus saw the crowds of people and had compassion for them. Why? Because they were harassed and helpless, like sheep without a shepherd. Then he said to his disciples, "The harvest is plentiful, but the laborers are few; therefore pray earnestly to the Lord of the harvest to send out laborers into his harvest."

Of course, a nation has a right to care for and ensure the flourishing of its citizens. But for those of us who are citizens of heaven, we have an obligation to also make room for the flourishing of others outside our national tribe—for we are not a tribe but a body. And as the body of Christ, we all have a part to play.

You have a part to play and so do I.

God has given each of us giftings, talents, experiences, and passions, and they're not all the same, so we'll each play a different part in serving and loving others around us. But if the body of Christ is functioning as it should, we'll all *together* be meeting the needs of various people and populations around the world. We can confidently choose to see and meet the needs of others because scripture tells us we're to function in this way. No one is trying to slow you up or distract you from the areas you feel called to engage with, but as the body, we should be aware of each other's pain points so when necessary we can support each other. This way of functioning together is essential to living out our beliefs about the dignity and sanctity of *every* human life. So the next time you see a headline that causes you worry or despair, check in with those who are involved in the work and who are proximate to the issues. I guarantee there's a way to jump in and help love the people caught in the middle of these stories.

Paul's story

Paul was from Cameroon, studied biomedical engineering, and loved the Lord. I asked him about Cameroon and what led him to come to America.

"I was granted asylum in 2002," he started.

He explained how in 1960, Cameroon became independent of France and Britain. Instead of Francophones and Anglophones moving forward to build a united country, the minority Anglophones soon felt politically and economically marginalized, had their language minimalized, and had their cultural differences ignored.

As a teenager, Paul was recruited to play in a prestigious traveling football (soccer) league, becoming a popular athlete who attracted fans and scouts, eventually landing a handsome contract to play professional football in France. However, a career-ending knee injury redirected his life in his late twenties. He returned to Limbé, his coastal hometown in

Cameroon's southwest region, where he enrolled in college and worked for a computer company.

Things at the computer company were not what they appeared. Paul was told his job was to draw up a census list using the company's database. But he soon realized the data was an illegal compilation of an electoral list for the ruling political party to draw up a rigging strategy.

It was clear the data would be used to bribe and disenfranchise voters and issue multiple ballots and electoral cards so supporters could use them numerous times. When Paul went to his boss to confront him with the evidence, he was threatened never to speak about the matter publicly. Paul resigned immediately and sought prayer with his family.

Despite his quiet nature and hesitancy to take action, Paul's faith guided him to do the right thing. He bravely spoke to local administrators of the joint municipal and parliamentary elections, revealing the voter fraud. He and others from the computer company who spoke out were soon arrested for "participating in secessionist and opposition activities." Paul would be arrested two more times and badly tortured before his family secretly put him on an airplane to the United States to seek asylum.[44]

Discussion Questions

1. Which "headline" do you most struggle with?
2. What was the most surprising information or story from this chapter?
3. Have other questions? Here are a few more answers to common concerns:

CHAPTER 8

how did I miss this?

I started this book with a sincere question: *How could I have missed this?* The answer is hard to talk about, because I *shouldn't* have missed this. When I comb through the screenshots of my life, the things I used to say, the justifications I used to make, I wince a bit. It's humbling to spend your whole life in the wheelhouse of Christianity and miss something that's so clear in hindsight—to miss humanity, compassion, and the kind of empathy that doesn't ask qualifying questions first.

The only way I know to answer honestly is to be deeply vulnerable about things that will make me (and others in my evangelical community) look . . . well . . . bad. I might even offend some of you. But at least it will all be out on the table for us to examine honestly—because I didn't miss this all by myself. I think the American church (in large part) is *still* missing it. I'm not finger wagging here. I'm in the same boat! We're all on a journey to better understand God's heart for immigrants and refugees. But as we get closer, the call of Christ will likely butt up against our carefully curated culture, our conscience, and especially our comfort.

When I started this journey, my question quickly turned from, *How* did I miss this? to *Why* did I miss this?

Lord, wasn't I in all the right places (church, mission trips, seminary)?

Maybe you've asked this question too.

You probably don't recall being taught to fear the stranger in Sunday school. So how did we get here?

Why have many of us limited our compassion toward an entire group of people?

When did we start justifying our indifference to their plight?

As I searched for answers to these questions, I gained clarity on how and why I think many of us missed it. Some of the realizations make me really sad, as I know the change that it requires of me—and that it asks of all of us—won't be easy or easily accepted. But I also have hope because I've experienced how freeing it can be to finally make course corrections that were nagging at my heart long before I knew what those whispers meant. Maybe you feel those naggings too.

So let's examine this together. Let's start by looking at some of the reasons why I (and maybe you too) missed this.

Reason 1: Rationing Compassion

Like many of you, I was born into the pews of evangelicalism. Our family was busy serving both in the church and in the community. Our table frequently hosted foreign exchange students and those with nowhere else to spend a holiday. Much of our lives was spent sitting with and befriending a variety of people from around the world. Yet while I was taught to love God and love others, *somewhere* along the way I learned to have a "healthy" skepticism of people, and in this immigration space, to fear the sojourner. For some reason, the stranger was someone to be kept at a safe distance. I was taught it was prudent to temper—and often withhold—compassion. Not *everyone* deserved mercy or care—at least until further context was known.

If we're not careful, we can easily fall into this mindset when we encounter anyone in a messy situation or broken livelihood. We tend to ask, Why is this person in this situation? What did they do to get in the mess they're in? (For example, asking for money on the side of the road, without a place to stay, or without a job.) My level of compassion used to be calculated from what I could reasonably know about a person: What effort they had put forth to get out of this hard situation on their own? Did they deserve to be in the situation they were in, or was it reasonable to extend compassion and concern? What avenues had they exhausted before getting to this place of desperation and vulnerability? If they had made bad choices or sinned, were they repentant and doing their level best to make it right?

If we're honest, many of us want to know if someone is trying to pull themselves up by their own bootstraps before we invest our empathy or sacrificially engage. And yet even though the Bible outlines a lifestyle of generosity toward others (Deut. 15:7–8; Ps. 37:26; Luke 6:38; 12:33; 2 Cor. 9:11; 1 Tim. 6:18–19; 1 John 3:17; and more), it somehow becomes all too reasonable to add these questions as caveats to our generosity.

I used to (subconsciously) feel better about limiting my compassion and empathy in the immigration space by over-simplifying the situation. People were in one of two boxes: *legal* or *illegal*. Compassion was warranted if you were in the right box. After engaging in dozens and dozens of conversations around the country, I've discovered these are popular boxes for many Christians and conservatives. Within these boxes are the preservation of things we value deeply: American culture and morality, social status, the economy and its resources, religion. All these important things *seem* to stand in conflict with Christlike welcome. And while preserving them isn't inherently bad, our prioritization of these values over the basic needs of others has inflated our fears and put significant distance between us and anyone who appears too different. The prioritization—even idolization—of these things has diminished our capacity to welcome. They become justifications for why we can't welcome. *Not yet*, anyway. If and when we get things in order, *then* we'll be better equipped, ready, and willing to welcome.

At least this is what I told myself.

Much of our culture conditions us to think this way, in a scarcity mindset, even when we have so much compared to the rest of the world. One of the biggest concerns I hear repeatedly is the narrative that "not everyone can come here." I admit, I also used to be concerned about this. If I was indeed trying to be compassionate toward those at the border, and loving people as I love my own family, what did that mean exactly? Did this mean I needed to be okay with "letting everyone in"? I already knew the pushback for this because I had heard it before: "Allowing everybody to come to the US would be a drain on the economy. While I'm all for helping people in need, if I don't make enough money to support my family, how can I help others? My economic stability allows me to be a generous giver. So it's important to put our economy and the needs of Americans first, right?"

It's an odd thing, is it not, to justify withholding good from someone until you can acquire and secure good things for yourself first?

While I'm not wishing anyone to be worse off, thinking this way does make us prioritize certain people: "our" people. It's the America-first mentality that we talked about in chapter 7. While it sounds reasonable on the surface, I'm quite confident this line of thinking won't hold weight when we stand before Christ.

I've spent some time looking, and I just can't find "America first" in the Bible. That's a hard pill to swallow (from a kingdom perspective) and an even harder reality to comprehend politically. I've learned this isn't an either/or conversation. *Of course* we're to provide for our families and ensure their flourishing. (This is why so many come to the US!) But I'm realizing we don't have to withhold flourishing from others in order to do so. We can start thinking, living, and advocating for the solutions that exist in the "both/and." The Bible tells us God will separate the sheep from the goats based on who loved their neighbors *as they loved their own children, their own family members, even their own lives.* According to this standard, do you think the King will recognize us? I'm convicted every time I read the parable in Matthew 25. It's quite the mind shift. A hard but holy heart check.

Conclusion #1: I missed it because somewhere along the way, I accepted the idea that some people in the world (for one reason or another) simply didn't deserve my *full* compassion.

Reason 2: Cultural Conditioning

I grew up in the throes of the culture wars of the 1980s. The Christian Coalition and Moral Majority made way for movements and events like Promise Keepers and Women of Faith. Conservative evangelicals were on an intense mission to "save the soul of America" by establishing clear gender roles in families and society, fighting against abortion and divorce rates, preserving prayer in public schools, promoting homeschool alternatives, speaking out against "the gay agenda," and pitching purity culture. The message was clear: we are pro-family, pro-life, and pro–traditional marriage. These things shaped the conversations we had in churches, at social events, and around dinner tables, and they cemented our political allegiances.

They were the things our Bibles and our trusted leaders told us were important. During these years it was made clear that conservative Christian issues were represented and championed by Republicans. Other social issues were progressive, part of the liberal agenda; we could never vote Democrat or have anything in common with people who were pro-abortion or favored gay rights. Immigration wasn't on our advocacy docket back then; if it was, I don't recall hearing much about it.

In the early 2000s, I was in high school and college, not paying much attention to anything in the news other than presidential elections. I remember conservative culture boiling with animosity as eight years of the Obama administration had us begging for something, anything, that would center our side of the culture war again. These years also brought about a new wave of campaigns evangelicals united behind, including adoption, modern-day slavery awareness, anti–human trafficking work, and renewed opposition to euthanasia. Feeding the poor, advocating for persecuted people around the globe, and taking care of those at the end of their life were never controversial topics; they kept us busy domestically and internationally (never forgetting our concern for abortion and orphan care). We cared deeply about these things and talked about them constantly. All of this defined who we were and what we stood for and against.

At the same time, migration to the US was seeing some interesting changes. From 1992 to 2004, unauthorized immigration increased, and legal immigration decreased. By the end of the period, more unauthorized than authorized migrants were entering the United States.[1] What was once a steady evangelical and biblical application of Matthew 25 to "welcome the stranger" soon became a prudent need to "uphold the law" according to Romans 13.[2] Immigrants (and their presence in our country) became defined not primarily as neighbors but as "legal" or "illegal," law followers or law breakers. We didn't know

how to see any gray area in between. This new differentiation—
and the attitudes prescribed toward each—marked much of the
evangelical discourse on immigration for the next two decades.[3]
While support for legal pathways to citizenship for undocumented immigrants increased, so did support for tougher immigration measures (a robust border wall, lower refugee intake
numbers, etc.).[4]

Then came the surprise rise of the Donald Trump administration, whose pro-life assurances and promises to protect
evangelicals came with contentious and inflammatory rhetoric about immigrants and refugees. By May 2018, a survey
published by Pew Research Center found that 68 percent of
white evangelicals—a group who had historically, staunchly,
and uncontroversially supported and welcomed refugees for
years—no longer thought the United States had a responsibility
to accept refugees.[5]

It seemed we evangelicals had a wavering tension between
our "missional desires and nativist fears,"[6] and the Trump
administration undoubtedly had us leaning into an America-
first agenda, blaming much of what we feared and what ailed
the nation on immigrants.

At first, I didn't pay much attention to the negative narratives racing back and forth between news outlets and political
parties. I wasn't anti-immigrant, and I didn't believe Republicans
or evangelicals were either. I believed every person was made in
the image of God. That said, like everyone else I knew, I simply
wanted people to come legally. But then I started hearing much
more than "come legally" from my Christian community. At
first our fears sounded justifiable—but our tone and conversations changed. Many believed the narrative that America
was being taken advantage of, that immigrants were coming to
exploit hard-working Americans. The idea made us increasingly
angry. Our rhetoric became dehumanizing, our dinner table

conversations downright icky. I couldn't believe what many in my community (myself included) were defending, what we were willing to accept about a group of people none of us *really* knew.

But immigration was deemed a progressive issue, one that threatened to uproot American culture and influence like any other issue in the Democratic platform. Advocating for anything in the immigration space meant you were for open borders and ignorant of or soft on MS-13 gang activity in cities across the US. As a conservative, I felt it was impossible to express curiosity about any other perspective. Immigration was a *political* issue after all, not a *biblical* one. This was a liberal issue, not a conservative one. These concerns definitely didn't fit in the pro-life space; that was strictly reserved for abortion and orphan care.

Any questions I raised were met with a clear and consistent line: This isn't the place for any *true* (theological or political) conservative to wander. It's a slippery slope, so step away from that ledge.

Conclusion #2: Another reason I missed it was simply my cultural conditioning. My culture taught me what to believe and who was worth fighting for—as culture always does. I didn't think we were missing something important. But we were.

Reason 3: Silence in the Church

According to a 2022 Lifeway Research study, when self-identified evangelicals were asked what influenced their thinking on immigration most, "the media" came in first, followed then by "the Bible." Only 3 percent said they were influenced by their church, and only 1 percent were influenced by national Christian leaders.[7]

Only 30 percent said they had ever heard discussions at church about immigration or were encouraged to get involved in outreach to immigrants or refugees. Yet over 70 percent of evangelicals said they'd value hearing a sermon that taught how biblical principles and examples could be applied to immigration in the US.

As evangelicals read their Bibles less and less each year,[8] what congregants hear on Sunday morning (or in discipleship classes offered during the week) becomes increasingly important. Seeker-friendly content tends to be the main competitor for the space necessary to disciple Christians in their biblical thinking and application to current (and usually controversial) cultural and social subject matters.

The first sermon I remember hearing about immigration wasn't in church but at a conference about biblical justice—and I was in my thirties. Without much discipleship and relevant application from the pulpit or intentional proximity through outreach and relationship-building with local immigrants or their congregations, our curious questions go unanswered by the church. When we hear and learn more about immigrants from our favorite pundits instead of our trusted pastors, we assume immigration is not a biblical issue but a political one.

Of course there have been pastors who have courageously found a way to speak to this issue in their churches, whether from the pulpit, in Sunday school classes, or by offering a week-night Bible study. And some have paid a high price for doing so. I'm thankful for their conviction to speak up for these forgotten image-bearers, as they try to reorient the hearts and minds of their congregants back to the main issue: people, not politics.

But sadly, 70 percent of churches are silent on the issue.[9] I believe our silence in the church will have ripple effects for generations, as Christians are being discipled more by cable news than by pastors. It's become a challenging subject to teach on or even to mention from the pulpit. As a pastor's kid, I get this, probably more than most. But I think we should be asking ourselves why it has become so difficult to address. Why don't congregants think of this as a biblical issue? What role has church leadership played in letting this get so far off the radar? While it's true that a pastor may have congregants for only an hour on Sunday, and cable news every other hour Monday through Saturday, the church's lack of discipleship has opened up a freeway of thought for the media to fill and frame. And frame it they do, dominating every lane of traffic, causing a traffic jam that enables many of us to stay all too safe in our comfortable and fortified echo chambers, unchallenged on this subject by God's Word or our Christian community. I encourage more pastors and church leaders to get on this highway (among others) and help clean up some of these roadblocks of false teaching, hateful rhetoric, and misguided attitudes that prevent so many from clearly seeing the way of Christ.

Conclusion #3: This silence in the church is yet another reason why I missed it.

Reason 4: Comfortable Echo Chambers

In 2022, after the invasion of Ukraine by Russian forces, people started messaging Women of Welcome and my personal inbox to ask how they could help Ukrainians. Once again, the pain of displaced families felt so far away and unfathomable—but people cared. One suggestion we made was to show solidarity with Ukrainians by simply showing up on a Sunday morning and sitting in the service of a local Ukrainian church. Yes, you could send something to a humanitarian charity, but we felt getting close to people was also important. Suggesting this to our online community felt disingenuous unless I did it myself, so I searched online for a Ukrainian congregation in Colorado Springs. I had such a lovely experience at a local Slavic evangelical church that

I started visiting other immigrant congregations in various parts of town. My very white and homogenous city started to feel quite colorful and multicultural.

One Sunday morning, my new practice took me to a Korean church just down the road from my house. The church met in a small building that doubled as a preschool. Parent announcements and offering plates shared the same counter space, and from the moment I opened the lobby door, I was met with grand smiles and warm hospitality. As I looked for a seat, I could feel every eye looking in my direction; I was the only blonde-haired, blue-eyed person in the service. "Don't be a distraction," I thought (a rule cemented in my brain from being a preacher's kid all my life). I spotted a row in the back with only two seats left. An older lady at the end of the chairs noticed I was sitting alone. She didn't speak English, but she smiled, handed me a bulletin, and scooted one seat closer to me. Midway through the first song, she handed me something from her Bible, a beautiful flower-pressed bookmark. Pointing to me, she signaled, *For you, from me. Keep it.* And she went back to singing.

As the hymns continued, I was noticeably a bit lost, as all the songs were in Korean. An older white gentleman (who looked as if he was married to the Korean woman next to him) walked over and handed me his hymnal. The inside pages had English on the left and Korean on the right. He turned to the page and pointed to the line I should be singing. He smiled at me before returning to his seat.

Being a guest at Christian services of other cultures, I was reminded of a book I had been reading called *Misreading Scripture with Western Eyes* by Randolph Richards and Brandon O'Brien. My entire life I've been reading and memorizing the Bible, so when I came across this book I was intrigued. "My goodness," I thought, "what have I been missing?"

The introduction of the book tells the story of a seminary

professor, Mark Allan Powell, who explored the cultural con-
texts that inform people's reading and interpretation of biblical
stories. Powell spent time in St. Petersburg, Russia, and gathered
fifty participants to read and recall the story of the prodigal
son. He had done a similar experiment with American students,
none of whom retold the significance of a famine as the reason for the son's return. But students who were from different
socioeconomic, ethnic, and religious backgrounds all recalled
the famine as an integral part of the story. Powell repeated this
reading and retelling activity again in Russia, and forty-two of
the fifty participants mentioned the famine. Why?

> Just seventy years before, 670,000 people had died of star-
> vation after a Nazi German siege of the capital city began a
> three-year famine. Famine was very much a part of the his-
> tory and imagination of the Russian participants in Powell's
> exercise. Based solely on cultural location, people from
> America and Russia disagreed about what they considered
> the crucial details of the story. Americans tend to treat the
> mention of the famine as a unnecessary plot device. . . . This
> is evident from our traditional title for the story: the parable
> of the prodigal (wasteful) son. We apply the story, then, as
> a lesson about willful rebellion and repentance. The boy is
> guilty, morally, of disrespecting his father and squandering his
> inheritance. He must ask for forgiveness. Christians in other
> parts of the world would understand the story differently. . . .
> The application of the story has less to do with willful rebel-
> lion and more to do with God's faithfulness to deliver his
> people from hopeless situations. The boy's problem is not that
> he is wasteful but that he is lost.[10]

The goal of Richards and O'Brien's book isn't to determine
which "take" on the story is correct but simply to raise the

question, "If our cultural context and assumptions can cause us to overlook a famine, what else do we fail to notice?"[11]

In all the years I've read my Bible and memorized hundreds of verses, I did so with two primary perspectives:

1. Consciously: the context of the original audience, time, place, and author
2. Subconsciously: my American worldview

It wasn't (and still isn't) my intention—nor the intention of any pastor, professor, or mentor that educated me—to "miss" any good and deeper cultural application. Context and historical application were the only ways I was taught to read the Scriptures. But more people than just white American evangelicals treasure and read Scripture. And to think that while I read the Bible in my own language, in my own cultural context, in my own kind of church community, it was "sharper than any two-edged sword, piercing to the division of soul and of spirit, of joints and of marrow" for *any* person, culture, or community around the globe. This bolsters my reverence for and trust in the Scriptures.

The Bible is a living, breathing account of God and God's people, and it buoys every soul that considers it. This includes the woman whose village was just ravaged by rebels, her family killed in front of her. This includes the father being forced into slavery to feed his family and prevent starvation. This must include those suffering from the terror and violence of beheadings for the sake of their faith.

The Bible seems relevant enough for me in my American culture and context, but to think of an even bigger movement of faith in all times and all places is sobering. To an American, the story of Ruth and Naomi can easily center on the great love story of Ruth and Boaz, but to others it is the journey of two migrant women working together to survive against all odds in a foreign land—what they had to do, who they had to be. We tend to center the story of Mary and Joseph on the humility and obedience of Mary to the will of the Lord, but others relate to the reality that these family members were minorities living in a region of violence, fleeing a manic dictator to survive. They can personally identify with the experience of Mary, Joseph, and baby Jesus as refugees on the run. How does this realization change our understanding of the stories we read?

We've memorized these parables and stories through the skyline of our own culture and personal experience. Our interpretation has remained quite fortified, and intentionally so. Let me explain.

We all can attest that Americans have grown more divided as the decades have passed. Social media has brought us together in some ways and torn us apart in others. Many of us now live (virtually as well as in real life) in curated safe places where we stick with people who agree with what we say, do, and justify. We are 100 percent right about our point of view and applauded for "standing strong" in our feelings. Instead of being renewed by the transforming of our minds (Rom. 12:2), testing and approving all of our lifestyles and relationships against God's will, we have wed spiritual fervor to our cultural fears. Because we live in these insulated community spaces, we repeat the same phrases without ever really experiencing life and people outside our echo chambers.

Conclusion #4: The comfort of staying in my own perspective and echo chamber is another reason why I missed it. At some point, if I want to be an effective witness for the gospel and engage the culture for Christ, staying solely in these places becomes untenable.

HOW CAN I TELL IF I'M LIVING IN AN ECHO CHAMBER?

Here are four indicators that I've realized firsthand:

1. I'm Easily Angered by Others

Example: I read a headline, or I post something and get a "detractor" in the comments mentioning a different viewpoint—and I'm ticked off. My anger is justified, right? It's "righteous anger."

Well, Christians tend to make the mistake of thinking all outrage is righteous, but sometimes it's not. Proverbs has a lot to say about anger, but Ecclesiastes 7:9 reminds us, "Be not quick in your spirit to become angry, for anger lodges in the heart of fools."

Often, in an effort to "want something better" for our country, our family, or our culture, we find our immediate response to others' opinions or experiences is an outpouring of frustration instead of gracious curiosity and compassion.

2. Most Everyone I Talk to Agrees with Me

"Not everyone does agree with me!" you might say. But the question is, Do people feel safe enough to engage with you honestly?

If you think yes, here's an example: I had a boss who constantly said healthy conflict and diversity were important. This boss always asked for "honest questions" during leadership staff meetings. But when people asked honest questions that required honest answers, my boss always roared back (and felt justified in doing so), belittling the question and accusing the asker of false motives and intentions. Soon people stopped asking hard and honest questions; the questions grew softer and the dialogue weaker. Everyone's hope for real conversation whittled away. And yet Proverbs 12:15 says, "The way of a fool is right in his own eyes, but a wise man listens to advice."

3. My View Makes Me Feel Superior

My island and everyone that lives with me here is right—and I feel good about that. I have the right viewpoint and answers and don't often welcome anyone telling me otherwise. There's really no nuance to be had. In fact, nuance is a dangerous word. You don't have to be close to people to create change; "*other* people" just need to open their eyes and get it. The world would be a better place if everyone just thought like me and my friends. And yet Proverbs 18:13 says, "If one gives an answer before he hears, it is his folly and shame," and Philippians 2:3 says, "Do nothing from selfish ambition or conceit, but in humility count others more significant than yourselves."

4. Labels Are My Friend

Anyone who thinks differently than I do has a label, and it's usually negative. People say that labels are lazy, but to me, they're key identifiers as to who can be trusted and who can't. And yet Titus 3:2 says, "Speak evil of no one, to avoid quarreling, to be gentle, and to show perfect courtesy toward all people."

These blind spots and echo chambers are crippling to the effectiveness and health of the church. Prayerfully consider these indicators, and maybe you too will realize something you've missed. Remember that Jesus wasn't afraid of outside narratives; he engaged them. He didn't lose his purpose, his zeal, or his ministry because he mingled with crowds of people who lived differently than the Torah had commanded. Instead, he was moved to compassion—and we should be as well.

How do I get out of an echo chamber? I must choose to love people well. It looks like this:

- choosing empathy over anger
- acknowledging people's pain
- listening instead of lecturing
- realizing labels *are* lazy
- prioritizing community over comfort

Reason 5: Proximity

When I first told my family I was going across the border to meet people in migrant shelters and street camps, they asked if I'd have a security detail. My mother was especially concerned: "Will you have bodyguards?"

I'm asked about this every time we (Women of Welcome and World Relief) invite people on our immersion trips to the southern border. I remember feeling this concern when I was first invited to Mexico, in 2017. I asked my colleague Sarah what she thought about it; she replied, "Well, I won't go if we have one."

"What?" I asked in astonishment. "You won't cross the border if we *have* security? Why?"

Sarah had crossed the border before and had some wisdom to impart. "It's just not the way you show up there. Walking among people who have no security, who are so vulnerable and afraid, it's just so . . . insensitive."

Walking through a tent camp in Reynosa, Mexico.

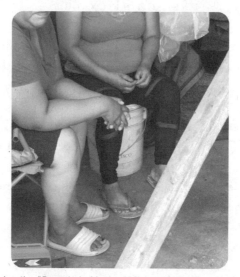

During the "Remain in Mexico"/Migrant Protection Protocol
program implementation, these women and their children have
been forced to wait in Mexico as they seek asylum in the United
States. We're sitting in a tent camp in Reynosa, Mexico.

I didn't understand. All I had ever heard was that these border towns were dangerous, cartel-run areas where violence took place every single day. I wanted to come home in one piece!

What I came to learn after several years of trips back and forth across the international bridge was that *I wasn't the vulnerable one.* I walked among these tarp camps and into shelter doors with incredible privilege. *Contrary to what I thought, I wasn't the target of the cartels or anyone else in these areas: migrants were.* People with no means, no provision, no community connections. There would be no national outcry or SWAT teams storming the streets if they went missing. There would be no involvement by national heads of state. No one comes for them. The truth is, the cartels make more money off vulnerable migrants when less government interference, cameras, and media attention are around. In general, they don't want to mess with Americans. It causes too much attention to things they wish to keep hidden. It's far easier and much more lucrative to exploit thousands of migrants and their families than a couple of random Americans. It's a reality I couldn't understand or even believe until I got close enough to see it for myself; the borderlands are completely different from what we see on the news. When you see it for yourself, when no one is creating a headline for you to click on or crafting a narrative to increase ratings, preconceived ideas start to fade. Black-and-white ways of thinking start to become gray. Proximity brings perspective. It changes everything.

In Christian circles, it's common to pray, "God, break my heart for what breaks yours," yet how many of us get face-to-face with the people and places Jesus told us he cares about, these places we know are incredibly broken? How can our hearts break if we never get close to the cracks people continue to fall through?

Walking into a church-turned-shelter in Tijuana, Mexico.

In his book *The Irresistible Revolution*, author Shane Claiborne surveyed a group of people who claimed to be strong followers of Jesus:

> I asked participants . . . whether Jesus spent time with the poor. Nearly 80 percent said yes. Later in the survey, I sneaked in another question, I asked this same group of strong followers whether they spent time with the poor, and less than 2 percent said they did. I learned a powerful lesson: We can admire and worship Jesus without doing what he did. We can applaud what he preached and stood for without caring about the same things. We can adore his cross without taking up ours.

> I had come to see that the great tragedy of the church is not that rich Christians do not care about the poor but that rich Christians do not know the poor.[12]

Someone shared this quote with me early on in my immigration advocacy journey, and I haven't been able to stop repeating Shane's words. They convict me—at times haunt me. Much of our American church culture is about helping the poor but not living with the poor.

But what does this mean? Are we all supposed to sell everything we have and move to the underserved parts of our cities? Are we not supposed to have nice things? The answer to this question will look different for everyone. It's not *necessarily* about not having nice things or moving to another area of town (although that is an amazing ministry that people and sometimes congregations have done). I think more important to consider is whether we're living near enough to feel people's pain, to know their individual needs, and to know how to truly love them well. We feed the poor, but do we *know* them? I suspect that once we know them, our own worlds and ways of investing will be challenged, and the Holy Spirit will convict us about what we should change to meet those needs.

The first time I heard anything of professor and author Ron Sider, he was on the suggested speakers list for the Evangelicals for Life conference I was planning for Focus on the Family along with the Ethics and Religious Liberty Commission of the Southern Baptist Convention. We were working to inform and disciple the evangelical community on holistic pro-life issues, and we were looking through our contacts to find the most knowledgeable people on a wide array of human dignity issues. We invited Ron Sider to speak about the connection between poverty and traditional pro-life issues. Since I didn't know who he was (a Yale PhD and a corresponding editor of *Christianity*

Today) I decided to preread his book *Rich Christians in an Age of Hunger*. In the very first pages, I read this:

> Can overfed, comfortably clothed, and luxuriously housed persons understand poverty? Can we truly feel what it is like to be a nine-year-old boy playing outside a village school he cannot attend because his father is unable to afford the books? Can we comprehend what it means for poverty-stricken parents to watch with helpless grief as their baby daughter dies of a common childhood disease because they lack access to elementary health services? Can we grasp the awful truth that eighteen thousand children die every day, most of hunger and preventable diseases?
>
> To help us image what poverty means, a prominent economist itemized the "luxuries" we would have to abandon if we were to adopt the lifestyle of our 1.2 billion neighbors who live in desperate poverty trying to survive on $1.25 per day:
>
> We begin by invading the house of our imaginary American family to strip it of its furniture. Everything goes: beds, chairs, tables, television set, lamps. We will leave the family with a few old blankets, a kitchen table, a wooden chair. Along with the bureaus go the clothes. Each member of the family may keep his "wardrobe": his oldest suit or dress, a shirt or blouse. We will permit a pair of shoes for the head of the family. But none for the wife or children.
>
> We move to the kitchen. The appliances have already been taken out, so we turn to the cupboards. . . . The box of matches may stay, a small bag of flour, some sugar, and salt. A few moldy potatoes, already in the garbage can, must be hastily rescued, for they will provide much of tonight's meal. We will leave a handful of onions, a dish of dried beans. All the rest we take away: the meat, fresh vegetables, the canned goods, the crackers, the candy.[13]

He continues with the bathroom taken apart, the water and electricity turned off. Then the house is gone. The family must move out to the back shed. Literacy is taken away as newspapers, magazines, and books are removed. One radio is left behind. Then government services of mail, hospitals, doctors, and nearby schools are removed. The family is left with five dollars.

Friends, can we understand this kind of living, this kind of lifestyle people are surviving around the globe and in other parts of our communities? How often do we put ourselves in a position to see these realities that we rarely encounter? If we're honest, we've become really good at knowing where to write a check. You and me both. Few of us have friends who live in such dire circumstances. We do a lot of donating, but do we ever walk or live alongside the people we're donating to? It's not wrong to attend the galas and write the checks. Ministries need funds. But when our money takes the place of our proximity to people, *this too* is how we miss it. I think Michelle Warren said it best in her book *The Power of Proximity*:

> Proximity to the poor is powerful. . . . Studying theology, sociology, anthropology, or policy is a great way to build your foundation as a person so you can better interact with the issues. But these actions are still limited. They keep you on the back of the bus away from the action. In contrast, proximity to injustice transforms your view of the bigger world and the people moving about in it. Most importantly it transforms you in all the ways that are necessary to help you take part in God's process of redeeming and rebuilding what is broken.[14]

Conclusion #5: I missed this because I prioritized my proximity to comfort, not to those who need to be comforted.

Who's to Blame?

So how did I miss this?

I didn't miss all this because my family didn't love people well. I didn't miss this because the churches I grew up in were unhealthy or filled with people who didn't deeply love Jesus. I didn't miss this because I avoided memorizing tons of Bible verses. I didn't miss this because my evangelical community doesn't care about people.

I finally found this—and it stuck—because they do.

I missed this because my worldview was grown where most people looked and thought like me. When I was growing up, it never occurred to me that there was a wealth of influential black and brown theologians who could also shape my understanding of Scripture and culture in deeper ways. I missed this because nearly everywhere I went, the environment was curated to be as safe and as predictable as possible for someone like me. Avoiding messy people, places, and topics was prudent; guarding your time and setting safe boundaries was idealized. I missed this because every mission trip I went on mostly centered on my experience and not that of the villagers we visited. We were always bringing God somewhere, to someone; sometimes we even thought we were doing the saving. Now I know God had always been there—I wasn't saving anyone; I was simply there to serve, to see, to learn, to fellowship. I missed this because for much of my life I saw differing groups of people only through carefully crafted media narratives and not through personal relationships. I now see how the danger of a one-sided story can affect generations of people. I missed this because my involvement with people who were in pain or poverty was a ministry of service, not the start of lifelong, lasting friendships.

Does any of this resonate with you? Does any of it make you weep, as it does me?

My goodness I have a lot to work on!

But let me say this: If you did miss this, you're not a bad person. You've likely just grown up a lot like I did. If so, the most redeeming thing about all this is that we were raised in a faith that is equipped to set sail. Staying on the shores while people flounder in the distance is no longer an option (if it ever was), not for those of us who really want to follow Jesus. It's past time to weigh anchor because we've been given a vessel that is designed to take on the wind and waves of any choppy and controversial waters ahead. People matter more than our pride, packed pew benches, or our politically partisan alignments. People matter more than any nagging doubts or tribal loyalties. I'll be honest, these waters aren't especially friendly. But you're not alone—there are shipmates present. And if we find ourselves afraid, we have a Savior in the boat with us, and as he has shown before, he is fully in control. We will become more like him as we wade into these waters.

Let's keep going forward together.

Let's follow Jesus into this space.

Let's not miss this anymore.

Carla's story

About seven years ago, already into her early fifties, something started to change for Carla. She had been a Christian since she was eight but says she was just content with going to heaven. When she decided to truly put God first in her life, the Holy Spirit changed her heart toward people. "I started seeing people the way God sees them, like I've never seen before," she says. Her views about immigration shifted as well.

She used to think, "Why don't immigrants who come to the US speak English? Why don't they try to become citizens?" God put a desire in her heart to know more, and she came across the Women of Welcome community. She started reading the posts on Facebook and thought, *This is me.* "It's been a big part of me ever since," she said.

She didn't know a lot about immigration before, just what she saw on TV. As she dove into the community, she read every book recommendation and watched every video she could to learn more. As she kept watching and reading, she saw articles about churches helping immigrant communities. Carla says, "I had to see it for myself. I didn't want to look away. I had to see it."

That is why she chose to go to the border in 2019 to meet people in the refugee camps in Matamoros, Mexico, with River Ministry, part of Texas Baptist Ministries. "I could not unsee what I saw," she says.

"When you realize these families are trying to survive, they're fleeing violence—it changes how you see them," she says of her time at the border. "The media tells us these are bad people. But when you see the women and children, when you see the fathers, you realize that's not who these people are. We have to get to know them and see them for who they really are, not who the media tells us they are."

The most challenging part of the journey for her has been feeling alone a lot of the time. Not all friends and family understand her changed heart. It's been a process helping some family members see where she's coming from. They ask things like, "Why can't you just do things for people in America? Why can't that be enough?"

"Many times we think someone else is going to do

that," she says, "and I've been there before. Where now, I see people how Christ does, and I have a placement on my heart about it." Carla says she loves America but sees how we've let ourselves be divided. "We have let politics become a part of our communities and church. I didn't see that before, and now I do, and it breaks my heart. When you take the risk to engage and help others, when you choose to be bold," she says, "it is so rewarding and such a blessing." At age fifty-eight, she says, "You're never too old to be used by God. It's never too late."

Discussion Questions

1. Bri frames this chapter around the question "How did I miss this?" What about you? If you've had a similar experience, what are some things you feel you missed?
2. Do you resonate with the conclusion Bri came to in this chapter? Why or why not?
3. Where have you learned the most about immigration? Is your church or faith community on this list?
4. Which topics does your personal "echo chamber" care most about? How does this impact your own values?
5. What steps can you take to branch out and learn more?

how can i help?

The number one question people ask when they get fired up about anything is, How can I help? If you're anything like me, I usually ask what the solution is and jump to making that particular thing happen. But anyone who works in the trenches of human dignity, pro-life, and social justice spaces knows solutions aren't simple. People are complicated, and systemic challenges are like layers of cement. If the problems were easy to fix, someone would have solved them by now. In these kinds of spaces, there are no silver-bullet solutions. If you want to get to the bottom of these kinds of things, you'll need more of a jack-hammer approach—it's going to take real work.

If we want to see lasting change, this work requires a long-game approach. Remember the anecdote from chapter 6: There comes a point where we need to stop just pulling people out of the river. We need to go upstream and find out why they're falling in.

Much of what I'm going to suggest in this chapter will feel far from the border crisis, but stick with me. It's a *both/and*. We need to pull people out of the river, *and* we need some hikers to head upstream. Both areas of work are important and necessary. In immigration, doing the work looks like serving and loving local immigrants who are currently drowning or have been washed ashore. It also looks like advocating for immigrants who are peering over the edges of the riverbank in their home countries and have yet to fall into the deadly swirls of the stream.

Counting the Cost

Before I tell you all the ways you can engage, I feel obligated to tell you just one more thing: Your willingness to help will cost you something, and it's likely something you're not accustomed to paying. I'm not just talking about a painful pinch to your wallet. It is a cost that might affect your willingness to move forward.

The first time I started speaking up about immigrants and refugees, a friend asked me to catch up with her on a quick walk. Midway down the neighborhood street she said, "I'm just gonna tell you, some of our friends are wondering what's going on with you lately. They've been reading your posts on social."

"What do you mean?" I asked.

"Well, Becka is wondering if you've gone liberal now. She thinks it sounds like you're going to vote for a Democrat. She's just a bit shocked that you're saying what you're saying these past few weeks."

Stunned and hurt, I stopped in my tracks. "I didn't say I was for open borders, and I didn't talk about voting at all. What is so liberal about wanting humane treatment for people showing up at the border? Shouldn't *all* Christians care how people, made in God's image, are treated?"

"I know, I know," she said, trying to calm me down. "Don't worry. I defended you."

She motioned me to keep walking.

I didn't.

Instead, I gave her a suspicious look.

"I did!" she exclaimed, waving me forward. "I told her I agree with you. I told her I liked your posts and that I understood what you were trying to say. She raised her eyebrows and then changed the subject."

"Why didn't she just come talk to me about it?" I asked.

She shrugged. "Well, you know how she feels about this stuff."

I slowly started walking again, head down. "Yeah, but it's me. She *knows* me."

If you live in conservative Christian circles and start talking about immigration or start getting close to immigrants and refugees, you might experience this same hiccup. You may feel alone and misunderstood. You might even get into a loud argument with your uncle, parents, or siblings. Don't be shocked if you do. You're not speaking up because you've been hoodwinked. There's no bait and switch in this conversation. I'm not trying to get you to "switch sides." Frankly, advocates are needed on whatever side of the fence you prefer, and that's the truth. So stay or switch, I don't really care.

People may wonder, "What's happened with you?" Well, you've hopefully just had some confidence attached to your compassion, and the Holy Spirit is telling you to start sharing. That's a hard thing but a good thing. It is a common experience for many of the women in our Women of Welcome community. We have a private Facebook group where women often come to find support. They've found the courage to tell a different narrative, read their Bibles in a fresh way, ask their friends and families honest questions. In response, some have been verbally attacked, shunned from gatherings, and unfriended.

I don't tell you this to make you afraid. I tell you this so you can be prepared. Speaking up will probably cost you something, but it's the right thing to do. Getting proximate to people will be messy, and explaining yourself will be exhausting, but it's the right thing to do. If anyone asks you why you're choosing to start welcoming "those" people, tell them you're following Jesus into this space for the flourishing of people and the glory of God. As a Christian, you want to show Christlike welcome and extend biblical hospitality. (That one is kind of hard to argue against, but sadly some people try.)

All We Can Do

The first time I spoke publicly about immigration was at a relatively safe place. I had been invited along with colleagues Jenny Yang and Tess Clarke to Dallas Baptist University to help students better understand what the Bible says about these issues. After the event, a woman came up to me who was noticeably not a student. She was about my mother's age and had driven over an hour to come to the event. "When I heard you were going to be here, I knew I had to come!" she said enthusiastically.

"That's so nice. I'm so happy to meet you! How did you hear about the event?" I asked.

"Well, I follow you on social, and I'm part of the Women of Welcome community!" she said.

"Wow, I love it. Are you connecting with others in the community, finding that helpful?" I asked.

"Oh yes, it's my lifeline! Do you have time for me to tell you a story?"

"Yes, of course. Please do," I said.

"Somehow I found the Women of Welcome account, and then I watched the *Who Is Welcome Here?* documentary you, Latasha Morrison, and Heather MacFayden were in, on YouTube, and I just bawled. I started watching every video you ladies have online. So when one of your immersion trips opened up, I applied for it but didn't get selected," she told me.

"Oh, I'm so sorry. Yes, those community trips fill up fast. There's usually a lot of interest," I explained.

"Oh, but when that happened," she said, "I couldn't wait for the next trip, so I gathered a couple of my girlfriends, and we went down to the border together. I had to see for myself what you all were talking about. It was nothing like I thought, but I'm so glad I went. I got home and downloaded every sermon outline and resource for my pastor from the Evangelical Immigration Table website and took it right over to him. My heart has been lit on fire, and I just never knew I could be so passionate about this!"

Watch the *Who Is Welcome Here?* documentary.

Evangelical Immigration Table website

This woman was beaming, and her energy was contagious. After we hugged and laughed a bit, I pulled her aside. "You said you went with friends, so I assume you're still okay on that front, but how's it been at home? What does your family think of all this?"

The smile slowly left her face. "That's been the hard part of all this. They're big Trump fans, and they don't understand what I'm doing. They're upset, wondering why I care about all of this now. It's been putting my husband and me at odds. I've gotten into a few heated conversations with my family. At first it was pretty bad, but now my daughter is starting to ask some good questions about it. So I'm hopeful," she said with a smile. "I'm just going to keep serving and doing what God has put on my heart. That's all I can do. I can't look away now." I had known this woman for only a few minutes, but she endeared herself to me right away. I was so proud of her courage and her determination to work through these hard dynamics.

In my twenties, when I was traveling the country working for the conference ministry Women of Faith, I heard author and Bible teacher Sheila Walsh say, "People will not always understand what the love of Christ compels you to do. Do it anyway." I hope that sticks with you as it has me.

If you choose to start with welcome, to just jump on in here, it's going to feel like you've chosen to go swimming on a good hair day (as my friend Michelle once said). But this is a worthy swim. You'll never have all the right answers. The rabbit trails you'll go down are endless. You'll likely cause some rifts in your safe spaces and relationships. But you're doing the right thing. There's no need for a cannonball your first time in these waters, but at least get your feet wet. We're doing this because our faith tells us to love others as we love ourselves. We're doing this because Christ has told his people to start with welcome.

Women of Welcome trip to the border: wrapping up a conversation with border patrol in El Paso, Texas. Pictured with: Chelsea Soblik (then with ERLC, now with World Relief), Elizabeth Graham (Stand for Life), Jamie Ivey, and Ann Voskamp.

At the southern border with colleagues Sarah Quezada
(Women of Welcome) and Tess Clarke (We Welcome)

What You Can Do

So how can you help?

Yes, I want you to click on the promoted wish list. Yes, please send that check—but more importantly, gear your heart toward welcome. Start there: with welcome.

Once you've shown up, decide to stay.

Even when it doesn't make sense.

Even when questions keep nagging and you don't have all the answers.

Even when it looks easier to engage elsewhere and you feel afraid.

Why stay? Because the Holy Spirit brought you to this point. And because nothing will change for hundreds of thousands of families unless we do, and that's an understatement. Christlike welcome is life-changing for those who need the invitation, but it's also life-changing for the inviter.

So yes, there are practical and tangible ways to help, which I'll share below, but most of the things I'm going to suggest aren't sexy or exhilarating. They'll likely make you uncomfortable and cause you to question yourself. They'll have you engage with people and places that are far from the strife at the border but are still core to the cause. You'll feel out of practice and maybe even a bit silly. You'll need to try some new things, and it will likely make you nervous, afraid even. You'll have to decide to do it scared. I've jumped off this diving board myself, and guess what? It was amazing.

Everyone wants to know, "What should we do? What's the *actual* solution?" Any time I'm asked this, I just tell the truth: "It's a combination of things, but honestly, what would help the most is immigration reform. Until that happens, we need to get busy caring about people."

At the end of the day, that's what's needed: immigration reform. When you hike upstream, apart from the regional governing dynamics and natural disasters that affect economies and communities, immigration reform is arguably the biggest challenge. And contrary to what most people think, the US president doesn't make immigration laws. He can make temporary executive orders or mandates about how current laws are interpreted, but when it comes to immigration reform, that has to be an act of Congress. So until we (the people who elect those in office) collectively hold our representatives accountable to work across the aisle and create reforms, most of the challenges we see downstream, at the border, across the globe, and for our immigrant neighbors in our communities, will continue to exist.

This is good news and bad news. The bad news is that neither you nor I can solve this problem. The good news is that we don't need to be so weighed down by the size of it that we can't pitch in to do work now. Until this act of Congress happens, the list of things we can do to help is long.

The Practical

How to help

There's a menu of things you can do to further attach confidence to your compassion and help our immigrant neighbors. It can be a bit overwhelming, so my best advice is to pick one thing to start with and stick with it. Simply start *somewhere*, and then follow your curiosity wherever it takes you.

If you're willing, let's go.

Prioritize Prayer

Without prayer, hearts become increasingly hard to change. One of the things I've learned in this journey is that there's one Holy Spirit, and I'm not him. I can say all the right things, and I can take on all the angry social media comments, but it's not my job to convince anyone of anything. Throw that pressure off your shoulders, and lay that right down at the feet of Jesus. It's our job simply to follow where God is leading, no matter how messy, hard, and controversial that might be. Welcome is a choice, and when other Christians understand that this is truly a biblical issue and not simply a political one, things will click for them too. One of the best things we can do is pray that people will see immigrants and refugees as *people* first, image-bearers worthy of welcome. "This is the confidence we have in approaching God: that if we ask anything according to his will, he hears us" (1 John 5:14 NIV).

You can pray for:

- The millions of forcibly displaced people around the world who are desperately searching for a safe home.
- Those making the hard decision to migrate to the US to help their family survive.
- Our Border Patrol agents who encounter thousands of people every month along our border. Pray for their safety, their support structures, their compassion, and for wisdom.
- Our president and other elected officials who advocate for policies and create laws: that they would do so with a kingdom mindset, working to ensure safe borders, compassionate and humane treatment of migrants, and more helpful legal pathways for families who need to flourish.
- Our communities to be welcoming to newcomers in our midst. That volunteers would show up and remain committed to helping immigrants and refugees integrate well into their new homes.
- Governments in unstable regions like Africa, the Middle East, Central and South America, Eastern Europe and Asia, and the Caribbean. Pray that God would bring about goodness and justice and that evil would be dismantled everywhere people are persecuted.
- The American church: that we would recognize this as a gospel issue and choose to teach, preach, and disciple the body to effectively show Christlike welcome.
- And that Christians would show up in new and fresh ways to serve those at the border, overseas, and in our cities.

Friends, as we pray over these specific areas day after day, *our hearts will be changed*. We will start seeing things we didn't see before—and encounter people we've never known were in our communities.

Keep Learning

The topic of immigration can feel like a minefield. You might be afraid that any step you take could cause all kinds of casualties. When you feel this way, remind yourself that you're not blindly following some fad cause. Jesus brought you here, and he's going to continue to help you take steps forward. "Whatever you have learned or received or heard from me, or seen in me—put it into practice. And the God of peace will be with you" (Phil. 4:9 NIV).

Becoming more informed certainly can help your confidence, so here are a few good reads and resources that can help you on your journey:

Books

- Academic, theology, policy-oriented
  - *Welcoming the Stranger,* by Matthew Soerens and Jenny Yang
  - *Seeking Refuge,* by Stephan Bauman, Matthew Soerens, and Dr. Issam Smeir

Helpful books

  - *The Bible and Borders* and *Christians at the Border,* by M. Daniel Carroll R.
  - *Refuge Reimagined,* by Mark R. Glanville and Luke Glanville
- Story or testimonial form
  - *The Stranger at Our Shore,* by Joshua Sherif
  - *Love Undocumented,* by Sarah Quezada
  - *No Longer Strangers,* edited by Eugene Cho and Samira Izadi Page
- Christian Worldview
  - *Thou Shall Not Be a Jerk: A Christian's Guide to Engaging Politics,* by Eugene Cho

- *Misreading Scripture with Western Eyes*, by E. Randolph Richards and Brandon J. O'Brien
- *Rich Christians in an Age of Hunger*, by Ronald J. Sider
- *When Helping Hurts*, by Steve Corbett and Brian Fikkert
- *Fearing Bravely*, by Catherine McNiel

Bible Studies

- Women of Welcome
  - *What Does the Bible Say about Immigration?*
  - *Christ-Like Welcome*
  - *Ruth & Naomi*
  - *Bold & Brave*
  - *Far From Home*
  - *In Pursuit of Peace*
- Other
  - *Making Room: A Study of Biblical Hospitality*, by She Reads Truth
  - *Arise: A Study on God's Heart for Justice*, by IF Gathering

Bible studies

Films and Videos

- Women of Welcome Resources (all found on our YouTube channel)
  - *Who Is Welcome Here* documentary
  - Equipping Series: educational videos on specific immigration issues
  - While in Our Care stories: testimonies of children in US immigration detention
- World Relief
  - E-learning workshops

Other resources

- Evangelical Immigration Table (specifically for pastors and church leaders)
  - *The Stranger* film
  - Thinking Biblically about Immigration video series
- Other documentaries
  - *Human Flow*
  - *Living Undocumented*
  - *Harvest of Empire*
  - *The Flagmakers*

World Relief
workshop

Get Proximate

This one will take some courage and maybe a little searching online. First, recognize that it's natural to fear people we don't know and to stay distant from what we don't understand. Fear has dominated the immigration space, and this has had grave consequences for immigrants *and* the American church. We've let our fears barricade us into "safe zones," socializing with "safe people" in "safe places." We teach and preach about "safe things." When Jesus walked this earth, though, he was having none of this from his followers. They were all going to walk *through* Samaria, not around it. Yes, it made the journey more complicated and their reputation more conspicuous. But Jesus wanted his Jewish followers to get closer to the very people they thought were unworthy. He wanted them to love these "outsiders" as true neighbors. They were image-bearers too.

Many of us look around our curated worlds and think, "I don't know any immigrants. I don't think I have any in my community either." But unless you live in an extremely remote area, you're likely driving by church buildings and small grocery shops that immigrants frequent. Sometimes you simply live on a different side of town from where immigrant populations have found community and settled. Start by checking if there's a World Relief office or affiliate in your community. If not, a simple online search of "local immigrant services in (your area)" can pull up some organizations and potential ministries to help you get plugged into serving, hosting, or meeting local needs.

Proximity is powerful, and it makes things personal. So what can you do to help? Get closer. Make it personal. We all show up to take care of our friends. When you can count some immigrants as friends, things will fall into place.

Advocate

This step is probably the most intimidating yet important aspects of how to help.

Your voice is needed in three main areas:

- In your spheres of influence
  By sharing content (like this book!) or thoughtful questions online or with friends.
- In your local church and community
  By encouraging your pastor and church leaders with what you've learned, giving them resources from the Evangelical Immigration Table, starting a small group with one of the Bible studies mentioned previously, or reading through *Start with Welcome* together.
- With your elected officials
  Don't worry; unless you have a direct appointment with your state representative, when you reach out, you'll likely leave a voicemail or talk with an intern who is simply there to take notes.

While the world has made immigration primarily a political issue, we now understand that it's also a biblical one. Much of what we're used to advocating for is personal. If our kids are sick, we talk with a doctor; if there's something happening at school, we schedule a meeting with the principal. We speak up to ensure that the supports and services our kids need are taken seriously. It's the same with our immigrant neighbors. This is why our proximity to people is so important. If you don't know an immigrant or aren't affected by any of the issues that surround the debate, nothing feels personal, and the urgency of the issue can get lost. But the Bible tells us to "speak up for those who cannot speak for themselves, for the rights of all who are destitute" (Prov. 31:8 NIV). No matter which candidate you prefer, no matter which way you vote, it's important to remember that rhetoric and policies affect people, and the flourishing of people is what we're after.

Not all advocacy is about shaping public policy; some of it is simply about challenging hearts and minds in your own home, helping others see and talk about immigrants as *people* first. In my experience, these kinds of conversations are much harder than calling your state senator.

I can already hear some of your fears creeping in. Yes, I'm giving you all this advice knowing you're not an immigration expert. Don't be too intimidated. Remember, you're an expert in your own journey of how God has brought you to this place. You're an expert in why you care about this and why you remain curious. Explaining why you have compassion is a great place to start. If someone asks you a question you don't know how to answer, it's fine to say, "I'm not sure about that, but I'll check into it and get back to you." Our culture has taught us to approach conversations ready to argue and win, but that's not what we're trying to do here. We just want to have a conversation about our compassion and how God has opened our eyes to something we didn't see before.

If you're looking for practical steps on how to use your voice well, here's a great resource to help you get started.

Using your voice

First Women of Welcome community member trip to advocate for vulnerable migrants at the US Capitol.

Standing outside the Russell Senate Office Building before we venture inside to meet with various senators about immigration reform. Pictured: Elizabeth Neuman (former G. W. Bush and Trump Homeland Security and Threat Prevention staffer), Matthew Soerens (VP World Relief), and Arturo Castellanos Canales (National Immigration Policy Manager).

Attending The National Immigration Forum's "Keepers of the American Dream" ceremony in Washington, DC. Pictured with colleagues Jennie Murray (Forum President), Jenny Yang (Sr. VP of World Relief, now with UNHCR), Tess Clarke (We Welcome Refugees), and Christine Sequenzia (then, with the National Association of Evangelicals), and Sarah Quezada (Women of Welcome).

Give

On the surface, apart from prayer, giving financial gifts seems like the easiest way to get involved, and those working to affirm the dignity of immigrants will tell you how much they depend on this kindness. The challenge is to give consistently and sacrificially.

> Now the full number of those who believed were of one heart and soul, and no one said that any of the things that belonged to him was his own, but they had everything in common. And with great power the apostles were giving their testimony to the resurrection of the Lord Jesus, and great grace was upon them all. There was not a needy person among them, for as many as were owners of lands or houses sold them and brought the proceeds of what was sold and laid it at the apostles' feet, and it was distributed to each as any had need. (Acts 4:32–35)

Giving generously weds us to people and places we might not have the bandwidth to pursue in any given season. Here are a few areas I suggest:

Invest in Home Countries

Much of the world's migration challenges are due to instability in countries and communities far from the US. Your investment in places outside the US can help shift local dynamics and even prevent people from being displaced or pulled into a dangerous migration journey. If you're looking to give to home countries, here are the things you should look for:

- Is the organization interested and invested in addressing the push factors in these regions: poverty, violence, and corruption?
- Do they have a community-level focus: business investments, education, leadership development, and anti-violence programs?
- Is the ministry invested on the country's national level: focusing on how to make government institutions stronger, reforming the justice and education systems?
- How long has the entity been serving in the region, and do they have any reputable US partnership affiliations?

Determining whether an organization's work orients around these kinds of systemic changes is a good practice. One of the best organizations I recommend in the Northern Triangle region is A More Just Society (ASJ: Honduras and AJS: USA). The work they continue to do in the region is incredible, and it supports the desire to strengthen the local community and government to eliminate the desperate need to migrate.

Giving in the US

There are two avenues to give here in the US: nationally and locally.

Nationally, it's helpful to give to education and advocacy organizations that inspire and equip people to live in closer proximity to immigrants and refugees. It's also important to invest in organizations that work programmatically in the US and abroad, directly serving people who are displaced. Here are a couple of places I recommend:

Advocacy and education oriented:

Donate to Women of Welcome

- Women of Welcome
- The National Immigration Forum

Programmatic and humanitarian services:

- World Relief
- Send Relief
- World Central Kitchen
- KIND (Kids in Need of Defense)

Giving locally is a wonderful place to start, as it will have you checking in and meeting people who are serving and resettling people in your city or county. If you don't have a World Relief office in your area, look for a local Lutheran Family Service, Lutheran Immigration and Refugee Service, or Catholic Charities that is helping resettle or feed newcomers to the community. Other places to check include Bethany Christian Services (who facilitates transitional foster families for unaccompanied migrant children) and of course area churches with specific ministry offerings and services for immigrant and refugee families.

Giving at the Border

Ministries run by those who work and live along the borderlands are on the front lines of receiving and caring for people who cross the border after traveling thousands of miles. They are the hands and feet of Jesus, and I couldn't sing their praises any louder. Investing in their work is incredibly important as those in need continue to come to these border towns. I highly encourage giving to these organizations, but it can be tricky to find the right one, as "pop-up ministries" along the borderlands are common, especially after a huge influx of migrants.

Here are questions to consider:

- How long has the organization been serving along the border?
- Does their ministry have a board of directors that holds them accountable?
- Do they meet ECFA responsible stewardship standards?
- Do they have partners they work collaboratively with in the region?
- Do they have relationships with area churches, national ministries, or denominations?

A few partners I have personally visited and wholeheartedly trust are:

- World Relief (Southern California office)
- Abara Frontiers (El Paso, Texas)
- Border Perspective (McAllen, Texas)
- Catholic Charities of the Rio Grande Valley (San Juan or Brownsville, Texas)

Women of Welcome: how to help

Again, here are a few more ways to help:

People First

Are you still with me? If so, bravo! That was a lot to get through. *There is much we can do.* There is so much hurt—and yet so many ways to help.

I hope after all the disclaimers and caveats, you're still willing to help. This kind of effort must be of your own choosing. But as my friend Jo Ann (who leads the Honduran office of A More Just Society) once told me, "Pick one thing and see it through. We can help bring about the kingdom of God. Give what you can, and see what God does." Jo Ann is one of many brave Christians in this space. She was living a safe and comfortable life in the US when she and her husband visited the Central American region on their honeymoon and fell in love with the people and the culture. After a few years of gaining more education in the US and learning Spanish, they decided to move to Honduras to help the region strengthen their communities and fight injustice, and they've never looked back. Little did they know they would help set up and fund school and healthcare programs across the country, restore local communities through national transparency and anti-corruption reforms (some of which helped purge over five thousand corrupt officers from the national police force from 2016–18).[1]

It's strange to follow God into places you've been told to fear, falling in love with people you never knew, people you were taught to keep at a safe distance. But immigrants and refugees are individuals made in the image of God and are deeply loved by him. If I claim to be a follower of Jesus, anyone who is deeply loved by God should be deeply loved by me too.

In her book *Start with Hello*, Shannan Martin tells of a time she craved real-life connection:

I am thirty-five, brand-new to the neighborhood, a shy introvert yet desperate to be known. I catch a glimpse of what life could look like if we all took one step closer to each other, unbothered by our differences. Slowly, I stop wishing to receive an invitation to belong and start writing my own. Unsure of where to begin, I set out to be the neighbor I longed for. This begins a decade of catch and release, where I take turns reaching out to the people close to me and they do the same. On paper most of us have little in common. But on sidewalks and along alleys we discover we want the same things: to trust and be trusted, to be seen and believed, to be generous. We want the security that comes with knowing we aren't alone in this disorienting world.[2]

Some of you might be scared to step forward. Some of you might be champing at the bit. It doesn't matter where you are on this journey, but in the days and weeks to come, it will be important that you don't stay where you are. Why? Because we are a pro-life people. We are a people who love God and want to do our best to love others, just as he told us to. The Bible is clear about God's creation: it's *people* first.

When I came home from one of my first trips across the border, I remember walking into church that next weekend feeling a dissonance I couldn't quite explain. I wondered if anyone would care about the experience I just had, the people I had just talked to and cried with, or the churches and shelters in Mexico that were asking for help. Would anyone else care about this issue like I was starting to? I sat off in the corner intentionally. With all my new and conflicting thoughts, I didn't feel like being around anyone. At the end of the service, I was handed a communion cup. The last time I had held a communion cup, I was standing against the wall of the US's southern border, hearing women and children through the cement slats as I asked for forgiveness, broke the wafer, and drank the juice. The weight of Christ's welcome was palpable as the scorching sun intensified my discomfort standing so close and yet so far from others in pain. Back home in my safe and comfortable surroundings, I cried through the invitation to eat and drink, sitting back in my chair without partaking. I didn't deserve such welcome into the family of Christ, into the citizenship of heaven. And yet Christ offered welcome anyway.

Visiting a section of the border wall when kids from the Mexican side approached asking for snacks or trinkets. I'm giving my "loved" necklace to a young girl.

After church, I tried to scurry off quickly, but someone I'd never talked to before abruptly stopped me. "You're Bri, right? I'm Courtney. Did you just get back from the border?" Stunned, I nodded. "Wow. Okay, a friend told me you were going, and I want to know what you saw. Can I take you out to coffee?" I agreed. Over the next week, I received messages from women in my church and city whom I'd never met before, asking to take me out to coffee to hear about my trip. Women were hungry to hear something true, hopeful, honest—something that would attach confidence to their compassion. I was so encouraged. I wasn't alone, and I promise, neither are you.

I have hope. Hope that the church will rise to her calling in all of this. Hope that her people will untether from their partisan platforms and pundits that so easily divide and prioritize proximity to people. I hope we stare long enough at the cross of Christ to remember that it was his death that welcomed us into a new life.

If we start anywhere, I think it should be here. Let's start with this kind of welcome.

Welcome one another as Christ has welcomed you, for the glory of God.

—ROMANS 15:7

Women of Welcome immersion trip participants learning from ladies who serve in a Baptist church/shelter in El Paso, Texas. Pictured with Jenn Jett Barrett and Pastor Sharon Miller.

A group of Women of Welcome ladies visiting a church-turned-shelter in Ciudad Juárez, Mexico.

Discussion Questions

1. What feelings, thoughts, or images are lingering with you after finishing this book?
2. What do you think about the idea that we're often more interested in talking about problems than doing something about them? Are there areas where that has been true of you?
3. Are you interested in taking tangible steps forward? If so, where would you like to start?
4. Bri talked about counting the cost before you jump in. What might it cost you to get involved more seriously with immigrants or refugees?
5. What is one thing from this book you want to be sure to remember?

acknowledgments

I'm often asked why I stay in this work, why I stay in evangelical culture. My response? It's my home, these are my people, my family . . . and I love my people.

And because someone came for me, helped me understand what I was missing, I'm forever grateful for the amazing people that invited me into this journey.

- World Relief team, Matthew Soerens, and Jenny Yang, your personal friendship and decades-long work in this space is inspiring and life-changing. Thank you for taking me under your wings, valuing me and this work.
- The graciousness and continued support from the National Immigration Forum, its staff, and its donors have made a bigger path forward for so many to enter this space. Ali and Jennie, thank you for your partnership and believing in this work.
- My Women of Welcome Team (*including Tim*), I couldn't do this without you, nor would I ever want to. Thank you for standing with me through my own journey and taking one with so many others in our community.
- Sarah Quezada, I'm forever indebted to your graciousness toward me. Thank you for being my friend.
- Michelle Warren and Cathleen Farrell, thank you for inviting me to see people like I never had before.
- Catherine McNiel, I couldn't have done this first book endeavor without your talent and collaboration. Thank you.

notes

Introduction

1. *Merriam-Webster*, s.v. "immigration," accessed July 3, 2023, https://www
.merriam-webster.com/dictionary/immigration.
2. Merriam-Webster, s.v. "asylee," accessed July 3, 2023, https://www.merriam
-webster.com/dictionary/asylee.

Chapter 1: How Did I Get Here?

1. Not their real names.
2. "Northern Triangle: Terrifying to Live In, Dangerous to Leave," World Vision,
November 2, 2020, https://www.worldvision.ca/stories/child-protection
/northern-triangle.
3. In truth, Christians have led sincere and beautiful ministries to immigrants
and refugees for decades. But after the heightened and inflammatory rhetoric
of the past decade, much of that work has been distrusted, discontinued from
approved ministry listings and promotions, and sometimes defunded.
4. Nicole T. Waters, "I Won't Look Away," *Women of Welcome*, 2019, published
at https://womenofwelcome.com/i-wont-look-away. Nicole's story first
appeared in 1029 at Mudroomblog.com.

Chapter 2: Is Immigration a Pro-life Issue?

1. *The Dignity & Sanctity of Every Human Life Resource Guide*, Focus on the
Family, 2016, 1.
2. Timothy Keller, *Generous Justice: How God's Grace Makes Us Just* (New
York: Penguin, 2010), 193.
3. Administration for Children & Families, https://www.acf.hhs.gov/; https://
www.adoptuskids.org/meet-the-children/children-in-foster-care/about-the
-children.
4. "Adoption Made a Difference," AdoptUSKids, https://www.adoptuskids.org
/meet-the-children/children-in-foster-care/about-the-children.
5. https://www.ncsl.org/Portals/1/Documents/cyf/Extending_Foster_Care
_Policy_Toolkit_4.pdf.
6. Mary Kaech, "Fostering Unaccompnaied Refugee Children: Part Two,"
Women of Welcome, Mary's story is taken from a longer version originally
published at https://womenofwelcome.com/fostering-pt2/.

Chapter 3: What Does the Bible Say about Immigrants?

1. *Evangelical Views on Immigration Study*, Lifeway Research, https://research.lifeway.com/wp-content/uploads/2022/09/Evangelical-Views-on-Immigration-Report-2022.pdf

2. Nicholas Wolterstorff, *Justice: Rights and Wrongs* (Princeton: Princeton University Press, 2008), 75.

3. "A Dreamer's Story: It's Our Job to Welcome Others," Women of Welcome, Nori's Story is taken from a longer version originally published at https://womenofwelcome.com/its-our-job-to-welcome-others/.

Chapter 4: Who Is Welcome Here?

1. Phillip Connor and Gustavo Lopez, "5 Facts about the U.S. rank in worldwide migration," Pew Research Center, May 18, 2016, https://www.pewresearch.org/fact-tank/2016/05/18/5-facts-about-the-u-s-rank-in-worldwide-migration/.

2. Erin Blakemore, "A Ship of Jewish Refugees Was Refused US Landing in 1939. This Was Their Fate," History Classics, June 4, 2019, https://www.history.com/news/wwii-jewish-refugee-ship-st-louis-1939.

3. "Observations Concerning the Increase of Mankind," 1751, National Archives, https://founders.archives.gov/documents/Franklin/01-04-02-0080.

4. Michael C. LeMay and Elliott Robert Barkan, *U.S. Immigration and Naturalization Laws and Issues: A Documentary History* (Westport, CT: Greenwood,1999), xxx.

5. History.com Editors, "U.S. Immigration Timeline," History Classics, August 23, 2022, https://www.history.com/topics/immigration/immigration-united-states-timeline.

6. "Irish and German Immigration," U.S. History, https://www.ushistory.org/us/25f.asp.

7. "U.S. Immigration Timeline," https://www.history.com/topics/immigration/immigration-united-states-timeline.

8. "The Immigration Act of 1924 (The Johnson-Reed Act)," Office of the Historian, https://history.state.gov/milestones/1921-1936/immigration-act?wpisrc=nl_aboutus&wpmm=1.

9. "U.S. Immigration Timeline," https://www.history.com/topics/immigration/immigration-united-states-timeline.

10. "Displaced Persons Act (1948)," Immigration History, https://immigrationhistory.org/item/1948-displaced-persons-act/.

11. "Mccarran-Walter Act Goes into Effect, Revising Immigration Laws," History.com, https://www.history.com/this-day-in-history/mccarren-walter-act-goes-into-effect.

12. "Refugee Relief Act," Immigration History, https://immigrationhistory.org/item/1953-refugee-relief-act/.

13. "U.S. Immigration Timeline," https://www.history.com/topics/immigration/immigration-united-states-timeline.

14. "Fidel Castro—Assassination Attempts & Facts," History.com, https://www.history.com/topics/cold-war/fidel-castro.

15. "Refugee Act of 1980," National Archives, 2023, https://www.archivesfoundation.org/documents/refugee-act-1980/.

16. "U.S. Resettles Fewer Refugees Even as Global Number of Displaced People Grows," *Pew Research Center*, October 12, 2017, https://www.pewresearch .org/global/2017/10/12/u-s-resettles-fewer-refugees-even-as-global-number-of -displaced-people-grows/.

17. "U.S. Immigration Timeline," https://www.history.com/topics/immigration /immigration-united-states-timeline.

18. "U.S. Immigration Timeline," https://www.history.com/topics/immigration /immigration-united-states-timeline.

19. This list was derived from multiple policy and government sources, mainly The National Immigration Forum website, and originally curated/written by Danilo Zak.

20. Glenn Kessler, "Trump's Repeated Claim That Obama Is Accepting 200,000 Syrian Refugees," *Washington Post*, October 8, 2015, https://www .washingtonpost.com/news/fact-checker/wp/2015/10/08/trumps-repeated -claim-that-obama-is-accepting-200000-syrian-refugees/.

21. Eugene Scott, "Trump's Most Insulting—and Violent—Language Is Often Reserved for Immigrants," *Washington Post*, October 2, 2019, https://www .washingtonpost.com/politics/2019/10/02/trumps-most-insulting-violent -language-is-often-reserved-immigrants/.

22. Washwire Blog, "What Donald Trump Has Said—About McCain, Obama, Immigrants, His Hair," *Wall Street Journal*, https://www.wsj.com/articles/BL -WB-56755.

23. "Trump on Twitter (June 18): Immigration, Germany," *Reuters*, June 18, 2018, https://www.reuters.com/article/us-usa-trump-tweet/trump-on-twitter -immigration-germany-idUSKBN1JE1FI.

24. "Trump Says the U.S. Will Not Be a Migrant Camp," June 18, 2018, Bloomberg, https://www.bloomberg.com/news/videos/2018-06-18/trump-blames -democrats-for-separation-of-migrant-families-video.

25. Linda Qiu, "The Context Behind Trump's 'Animals' Comment," May 18, 2018, https://www.nytimes.com/2018/05/18/us/politics/fact-check-trump -animals-immigration-ms13-sanctuary-cities.html.

26. "President Donald Trump Lashes Out at Immigrants," Ebru Television, January 12, 2018, https://ebru.co.ke/president-donald-trump-lashes-out-at -immigrants/.

27. "Muslim Travel Ban," Immigration History, https://immigrationhistory.org /item/muslim-travel-ban/.

28. "U.S. Annual Refugee Resettlement Ceilings and Number of Refugees Admitted, 1980-Present," Migration Policy, https://www.migrationpolicy.org /programs/data-hub/charts/us-refugee-resettlement.

29. Akmal Dawi, "The Massive, Costly Afghan Evacuation in Numbers," *Voice of America (VOA)*, February 18, 2022, https://www.voanews.com/a/the-massive -costly-afghan-evacuation-in-numbers/6449553.html.

30. Juhohn Lee, "American Has Spent over a Trillion Dollars Fighting the War on Drugs. 50 Years Later, Drug Use in the U.S. Is Climbing Again," CNBC, June 17, 2021, https://www.cnbc.com/2021/06/17/the-us-has-spent-over-a-trillion -dollars-fighting-war-on-drugs.html.

31. Kristen Bialik, "Border Apprehensions Increased in 2018—Especially for

Migrant Families," Pew Research Center, January 16,2019, https://www
.pewresearch.org/fact-tank/2019/01/16/border-apprehensions-of-migrant
-families-have-risen-substantially-so-far-in-2018/.

32. Stephen P. Wood, "The Intersection of Human Trafficking and Immigration,"
Bill of Health (blog), June 27, 2018, https://blog.petrieflom.law.harvard.edu
/2018/06/27/the-intersection-of-human-trafficking-and-immigration/.

33. "Governor Ron DeSantis Takes Action to Protect Floridians from the
Dangerous Impacts of the Biden Border Crisis," *Ron DeSantis News Releases*,
September 28, 2021, https://www.flgov.com/2021/09/28/governor-ron
-desantis-takes-action-to-protect-floridians-from-the-dangerous-impacts-of
-the-biden-border-crisis/.

34. Harrison Ray, "Fox News Fearmongered about Migrants and the Immigration
System in at Least 693 Segments in a 12-Week Period," Media Matters for
America, June 30, 2021, https://www.mediamatters.org/fox-news/fox-news
-fearmongered-about-migrants-and-immigration-system-least-693-segments
-12-week.

35. Camilo Montoya-Galvez, "U.S. to Extend Legal Stay of Ukrainian Refuges
Processed along Mexican Border," CBS News, https://www.cbsnews.com
/news/ukrainian-refugees-us-extends-legal-stay-mexico-border/.

36. Herb Scribner, "U.S. Admits 100,000 Ukrainians in 5 Months," Axios, July
29, 2022, https://www.axios.com/2022/07/29/ukraine-refugees-united-states
-numbers.

37. Ray, "Fox News fearmongered about migrants," https://www.mediamatters.org
/fox-news/fox-news-fearmongered-about-migrants-and-immigration-system
-least-693-segments-12-week.

38. Lisa's story is taken from a longer version originally published at https://women
ofwelcome.com/what-kind-of-neighbor-do-you-want-to-be/.

Chapter 5: What Does Christlike Welcome Look Like?

1. "108.4 Million People Worldwide Were Forcibly Displaced," UNHCR Figures
At A Glance, June 14, 2023, https://www.unhcr.org/us/about-unhcr/who-we
-are/figures-glance.

2. "108.4 Million People," https://www.unhcr.org/en-us/figures-at-a-glance.html.

3. This is a slightly redacted version of the original story found at the website.
(You can listen to more sworn testimonies of these children on Women of
Welcome's website, WomenofWelcome.com/WhileinOurCare, or at The
Flores Exhibits' website, flores-exhibits.org)

4. "The Trump Administration's 'Zero Tolerance' Immigration Enforcement
Policy," Congressional Research Service, February 2, 2021, https://crsreports
.congress.gov/product/pdf/R/R45266.

5. *Review of the Department of Justice's Planning and Implementation of Its Zero
Tolerance Policy and Its Coordination with the Departments of Homeland Security
and Health and Human Services*, Department of Justice, January 2021, https://
oig.justice.gov/sites/default/files/reports/21-028_0.pdf; "Senate Judiciary
Questions Ramification Plan—At The Breaking Point: The Humanitarian and
Security Crisis at our Southern Border," https://www.judiciary.senate.gov
/imo/media/doc/Provost%20Responses%20to%20QFRs1.pdf.

6. "Senate Judiciary Questions Ramification Plan," https://www.judiciary.senate
   .gov/imo/media/doc/Provost%20Responses%20to%20QFRs1.pdf.
7. "The Trump Administration's Zero Tolerance,'" https://crsreports.congress
   .gov/product/pdf/R/R45266, first page, last paragraph.
8. "In the Freezer-Abusive Conditions for Women and Children in US
   Immigration Holding Cells," Human Rights Watch (HRW), February 28,
   2018, https://www.hrw.org/report/2018/02/28/freezer/abusive-conditions
   -women-and-children-us-immigration-holding-cells.
9. Julia Ainsley and Jacob Soboroff, "Trump Cabinet Officials voted in 2018
   White House meeting to separate migrant children, say officials," NBC News,
   August 20, 2020, https://www.nbcnews.com/politics/immigration/trump
   -cabinet-officials-voted-2018-white-house-meeting-separate-migrant-n1237416.
10. "Trump Migrant Separation Policy: Children 'in Cages' in Texas," BBC News,
    June 18, 2018, https://www.bbc.com/news/world-us-canada-44518942.
11. "Exhibits #3 through #69," *The Flores Exhibits*, https://flores-exhibits.org/.
12. "Exhibits #3 through #69," https://flores-exhibits.org/.
13. The idea of God as a prodigal father is explained in detail in Timothy Keller's
    The Prodigal God and elsewhere.
14. Sherene's story is taken from a longer version originally published at "Sherene
    Joseph, "Whom Can You Invited to Sit at Your Holiday Table?," Women of
    Welcome, 2023, https://womenofwelcome.com/invite-holiday-table/.

Chapter 6: Why Do People Come?

1. Country changed for safety reasons.
2. "Questions and Answers: Credible Fear Screening," U.S. Citizenship and
   Immigration Services, July 26, 2023, https://www.uscis.gov/humanitarian
   /refugees-and-asylum/asylum/questions-and-answers-credible-fear-screening.
3. Metering began with Haitians in Tijuana under Obama in 2016, albeit for
   only a short time before it was stopped.
4. "Push or Pull Factors: What Drives Central American Migrants to the U.S.?,"
   National Immigration Forum, July 23, 2019, https://immigrationforum.org
   /article/push-or-pull-factors-what-drives-central-american-migrants-to-the-u
   -s/#_ftn1.
5. Jo Ann Van Engen, "Helping People in Their Home Countries," Women
   of Welcome, August 23, 2022, YouTube video, 50:37, https://youtu.be/1o
   -QB6YhVK0.
6. Abby Budiman, "Key Findings about U.S. Immigrants," Pew Research Center,
   August 20, 2020, https://www.pewresearch.org/fact-tank/2020/08/20/key
   -findings-about-u-s-immigrants/.
7. Lynsey Addario, "Pregnant, Exhausted and Turned Back at the Border," *New
   York Times*, November 27, 2020, https://www.nytimes.com/2020/11/27/us
   /border-mexico-pregnant-women.html.
8. "Webinar Series—Root Causes of Migration," Justice for Immigrants, https://
   justiceforimmigrants.org/uncategorized/webinar-series-root-causes-of
   -migration.
9. Rodrigo Dominguez Villegas, "Central American Migrants and 'La Bestia':
   The Route, Dangers, and Government Responses," September 10, 2014,

Migration Policy Institute, https://www.migrationpolicy.org/article/central
-american-migrants-la-bestia.

10. Judy Woodruff with Nick Schifrin, "Migrants Risk the Dangerous Trip to the
U.S. Because It Is Safer than Staying Home," PBS News Hour, June 20, 2018,
https://www.pbs.org/newshour/show/migrants-risk-the-dangerous-trip-to-the
-u-s-because-its-safer-than-staying-home.

11. Woodruff and Schifrin, "Migrants Risk the Dangerous Trip," https://www.pbs
.org/newshour/show/migrants-risk-the-dangerous-trip-to-the-u-s-because-its
-safer-than-staying-home.

12. Sarah Quezada, "10 Things Christians Should Know about Immigration,"
Crosswalk.com, July 17, 2018, https://www.crosswalk.com/faith/spiritual-life
/10-things-christians-should-know-about-immigration.html

13. "Diversity Visa Program, DV 2019-2021: Number of Entries During Each
Online Registration Period by Region and Country of Chargeability," U.S.
Department of State, https://travel.state.gov/content/dam/visas/Diversity
-Visa/DVStatistics/DV-applicant-entrants-by-country-2019-2021.pdf.

14. "Asylum Decisions," TRAC Immigration, https://trac.syr.edu/phptools
/immigration/asylum/.

Chapter 7: Have You Seen This Headline?

1. Eleanor Goldberg, "80% of Central American Women, Girls Are Raped
Crossing Into The U.S.," HuffPost, December 6, 2017, https://www.huffpost
.com/entry/central-america-migrants-rape_n_5806972.

2. Camilo Montoya-Galvez, "The Facts behind the High Number of Migrants
Arriving at the Border under Biden," CBS News, August 31, 2022, https://
www.cbsnews.com/news/immigration-biden-us-mexico-border/.

3. Julia Jacobo and Anne Laurent, "Migrant Other Seeing Fleeing Tear Gas
with Children: 'I Felt I Was Going to Die'," ABC News, November 28, 2018,
https://abcnews.go.com/International/felt-die-migrant-mother-fleeing-tear
-gas-children/story?id=59456810.

4. "U.S. Customs and Border Protection Budget Overview," Department of
Homeland Security, Fiscal Year 2023, https://www.dhs.gov/sites/default/files
/2022-03/U.S.%20Customs%20and%20Border%20Protection_Remediated
.pdf#page=40.

5. "Total Illegal Alien Apprehensions By Month - FY 2000–2019," United States
Border Patrol, 2019, https://www.cbp.gov/sites/default/files/assets/documents
/2020-Jan/U.S.%20Border%20Patrol%20Monthly%20Apprehensions%20
%28FY%202000-%20FY%202019%29_1.pdf.

6. "DHS Border Security Metrics Report," Department of Homeland Security,
August 5, 2020, https://www.dhs.gov/sites/default/files/publications
/immigration-statistics/BSMR/ndaa_border_security_metrics_report_fy
_2019_0.pdf.pdf#page=16.

7. Lauren Giella, "Fact Check: Is the U.S.-Mexico Border More Secure Than
Ever, as Trump Says?", Newsweek 90, January 13, 2021, https://www.newsweek
.com/fact-check-us-mexico-border-more-secure-ever-trump-says-1561303;
Dr. Russell Moore and Bri Stensrud, "Border Security," Women of Welcome
Equipping Series, https://youtu.be/3xRox8BRXbA?si=u-hwhuoduWYyUS3F.

8. Elizabeth Neumann, "Amid Afghanistan chaos, refugee vetting process is sound: OPNION," *ABC News*, August 28, 2021, https://abcnews.go.com/International/amid-afghanistan-chaos-refugee-vetting-process-sound-opinion/story?id=79689151; "Rigorous Refugee Vetting Process for the U.S.," Center for Victims of Torture, August 2, 2023, https://www.cvt.org/Refugee-Vetting-Process.

9. https://storymaps.esri.com/stories/2016/refugee-camps/.

10. https://www.brookings.edu/blog/order-from-chaos/2018/06/19/when-refugee-displacement-drags-on-is-self-reliance-the-answer/; https://www.wvi.org/opinion/view/working-together-refugees-not-exactly-what-you-think-it.

11. https://www.cvt.org/Refugee-Vetting-Process.

12. Matthew Soerens and Jenny Yang, *Welcoming the Stranger: Justice, Compassion & Truth in the Immigration Debate* (Downers Grove, IL: InterVarsity Press), 107.

13. "Inside the World's 10 Largest Refugee Camps," UNHCR-The UN Refugee Agency, https://www.cvt.org/Refugee-Vetting-Process.

14. "FACT SHEET: Asylum in the United States," American Immigration Council, August 16, 2022, https://www.americanimmigrationcouncil.org/research/asylum-united-states.

15. "FACT SHEET: Asylum Fraud and Immigration Court Absentia Rates," National Immigration Forum, October 2021, https://immigrationforum.org/article/fact-sheet-asylum-fraud-and-immigration-court-absentia-rates/.

16. Ilona Bray, "How USCIS Spots Fraud in an Asylum Application," *NOLO*, https://www.nolo.com/legal-encyclopedia/how-uscis-spots-fraud-find-asylum-application.html.

17. "FACT SHEET: Asylum Fraud and Immigration Court Absentia Rates," https://immigrationforum.org/article/fact-sheet-asylum-fraud-and-immigration-court-absentia-rates/.

18. Soerens and Yang, *Welcoming the Stranger*, 107.

19. Soerens and Yang, *Welcoming the Stranger*, 107.

20. Richard Gonzales, "For 7th Consecutive Year, Visa Overstays Exceeded Illegal Border Crossings," National Public Radio, January 16, 2019, https://www.npr.org/2019/01/16/686056668/for-seventh-consecutive-year-visa-overstays-exceeded-illegal-border-crossings.

21. Tim Arnett, "Illegal Immigrants and the Economy," *Wall Street Journal*, April 13, 2006, https://www.wsj.com/articles/SB114477669441223067.

22. "Asylum," U.S. Citizenship and Immigration Services, July 31, 2023, https://www.uscis.gov/humanitarian/refugees-and-asylum/asylum.

23. Stephen Moore, "A Fiscal Portrait of the Newest Americans," National Immigration Forum and the Cato Institute, July 1998, https://files.eric.ed.gov/fulltext/ED427118.pdf.

24. Soerens and Yang, *Welcoming the Stranger*, 130.

25. Daniel E. Martinez and Ruben G. Rumbaut, "The Criminalization of Immigration in the United States, American Immigration Council, July 13, 2015, https://www.americanimmigrationcouncil.org/research/criminalization-immigration-united-states.

26. Alex Nowrasteh, "Terrorism and Immigration: A Risk Analysis," CATO

Institute, September 13, 2016, https://www.cato.org/policy-analysis/terrorism-immigration#conclusion.

27. "Common Questions," Women of Welcome, https://womenofwelcome.com/common-questions/.

28. Hannah Dreier, "I've Been Reporting on MS-13 for a Year: Here Are the 5 Things Trump Gets Most Wrong," PropPublica, June 25, 2018, https://www.propublica.org/article/ms-13-immigration-facts-what-trump-administration-gets-wrong.

29. Sarah Kinosian, "Seven Facts about MS-13 and How to Combat the Gang," WOLA, July 18, 2017, https://www.wola.org/analysis/ms-13-not-immigration-problem/.

30. "Fact Sheet: Immigrant Youth and MS-13," Law Enforcement Immigration Task Force, December 12, 2017, https://leitf.org/2017/12/fact-sheet-immigrant-youth-ms-13/.

31. Kinosian, "Seven Facts about MS-13," https://www.wola.org/analysis/ms-13-not-immigration-problem/.

32. "Fact Sheet: Immigrant Youth and MS-13," https://leitf.org/2017/12/fact-sheet-immigrant-youth-ms-13./

33. Dreier, "I've Been Reporting," https://www.propublica.org/article/ms-13-immigration-facts-what-trump-administration-gets-wrong.

34. "What Is Sharia Law? What Does It Mean for Women in Afghanistan?," BBC, August 19, 2021, https://www.bbc.com/news/world-27307249.

35. Melissa Block, host, "Religious Laws Long Recognized by U.S. Courts," National Public Radio, September 8, 2010, https://www.npr.org/transcripts/129731015.

36. Brian Montopoli, "Fears of Sharia Law in America Grow among Conservatives," CBS News, October 13, 2010, https://www.cbsnews.com/news/fears-of-sharia-law-in-america-grow-among-conservatives/.

37. First Amendment of the US Constitution: Congress shall make no law respecting an establishment of religion, or prohibiting the free exercise thereof; or abridging the freedom of speech, or of the press; or the right of the people peaceably to assemble, and to petition the Government for a redress of grievances.

38. "Human Trafficking: Modern Enslavement of Immigrant Women in the United States," ACLU, May 31, 2007, https://www.aclu.org/documents/human-trafficking-modern-enslavement-immigrant-women-united-states.

39. "Human Trafficking: Modern Enslavement," https://www.aclu.org/other/human-trafficking-modern-enslavement-immigrant-women-united-states.

40. "Human Trafficking," U.S. Customs and Border Protection, https://www.cbp.gov/border-security/human-trafficking.

41. Hailey York, "U.S. Immigration Police and Human Trafficking: Two Sides of the Same Coin," Human Trafficking Institute, August 11, 2022, https://traffickinginstitute.org/u-s-immigration-policy-and-human-trafficking-two-sides-of-the-same-coin/.

42. Joel Rose, "Many Americans Falsely Think Migrants Are Bringing Most of the Fentanyl Entering U.S.," National Public Radio, August 18, 2022, https://www.npr.org/2022/08/18/1118271910/many-americans-falsely-think-migrants-are-bringing-most-of-the-fentanyl-entering.

43. Rose, "Many Americans Falsely Think," https://www.npr.org/2022/08/18/1117953720/a-majority-of-americans-see-an-invasion-at-the-southern-border-npr-poll-finds.

44. Cara Salazar, "Why Do Asylum Seekers Leave Their Countries and Come to the U.S.," *Women of Welcome.*, https://womenofwelcome.com/why-do-asylum-seekers-leave/. Paul's story is taken from a longer version originally published on this website.

Chapter 8: How Did I Miss This?

1. Jeffrey S. Passel and Roberto Suro, "Rise, Peak, and Decline: Trends in U.S. Immigration 1992–2004," Pew Research Center, September 27, 2005, https://www.pewresearch.org/hispanic/2005/09/27/rise-peak-and-decline-trends-in-us-immigration-1992-2004/.

2. Ulrike Elisabeth Stockhausen, *The Strangers in our Midst: American Evangelicals and Immigration from the Cold War to the TwentyFirst Century* (Oxford University Press, 2021).

3. Stockhausen, *The Strangers in our Midst.*

4. Stockhausen, *The Strangers in our Midst.*

5. Hannah Hartig, "Republicans Turn More Negative toward Refugees as Number Admitted to U.S. Plummets," May 24, 2018, Pew Research Center, https://www.pewresearch.org/short-reads/2018/05/24/republicans-turn-more-negative-toward-refugees-as-number-admitted-to-u-s-plummets/.

6. Stockhausen, *The Strangers in our Midst*, 5.

7. "Evangelical Views on Immigration: A Survey of Americans," Lifeway Research, https://research.lifeway.com/wp-content/uploads/2022/09/Evangelical-Views-on-Immigration-Report-2022.pdf, page 70.

8. Adam Macinnis, "Report: 26 Million Americans Stopped Reading the Bible Regularly During COVID-19," *Christianity Today*, April 20, 2022, https://www.christianitytoday.com/news/2022/april/state-of-bible-reading-decline-report-26-million.html.

9. "Evangelical Views on Immigration," https://research.lifeway.com/wp-content/uploads/2022/09/Evangelical-Views-on-Immigration-Report-2022.pdf.

10. E. Randolph Richards and Brandon J. O'Brien, *Misreading Scripture with Western Eyes* (Downers Grove, IL: InterVarsity Press, 2013), 14–15.

11. Richards and O'Brien, *Misreading Scripture with Western Eyes*, 14–15.

12. Shane Claiborne, *The Irresistible Revolution: Living as an Ordinary Radical* (Grand Rapids: Zondervan, 2006), 70.

13. Ron Sider, *Rich Christians in an Age of Hunger* (Nashville: Word, 1997, 2015), 3.

14. Michelle Warren, *The Power of Proximity* (Downers Grove: InterVarsity Press, 2017), 7–8.

Chapter 9: How Can I Help?

1. "Purging And Transformation of the Honduran National Police Force," Association for a More Just Society (ASJ), February 18, 2019, https://www.asj-us.org/stories/security/purging-and-transformation-of-the-honduran-national-police-force.

2. Shannan Martin, *Start with Hello* (Grand Rapids: Revell, 2022), 13.